ZERO TO 60

A Teen's Guide to Manage
Frustration, Anger, and
Everyday Irritations

MICHAEL A. TOMPKINS, PHD, ABPP

ILLUSTRATED BY CHLOE DOUGLASS

Magination Press • Washington, DC • American Psychological Association

For Mady and Livie,
who never go from zero to 60 in seconds but cruise along at
the speed limit (mostly).

Books for Kids From the
American Psychological Association
maginationpress.org

Text copyright © 2020 by Magination Press, an imprint of the American Psychological Association. Illustrations copyright © 2020 by Chloe Douglass. Published in 2020 by Magination Press. All rights reserved. Except as permitted under the United States Copyright Act of 1976, no part of this publication may be reproduced or distributed in any form or by any means, or stored in a database or retrieval system, without the prior written permission of the publisher.

Magination Press is a registered trademark of the American Psychological Association. Order books at maginationpress.org, or call 1-800-374-2721.

Book design by Rachel Ross

Cover printed by Phoenix Color, Hagerstown, MD
Interior printed by Sheridan Books, Inc., Chelsea, MI

Library of Congress Cataloging-in-Publication Data

Names: Tompkins, Michael A., author.
Title: Zero to 60: a teen's guide to manage frustration, anger, and
    everyday irritations/Michael A. Tompkins, PhD, ABPP.
Other titles: Zero to sixty
Description: Washington, DC: Magination Press, [2020] | Includes
    bibliographical references and index.
Identifiers: LCCN 2020013654 | ISBN 9781433832475 (paperback)
Subjects: LCSH: Anger in adolescence—Juvenile literature. |
    Calmness—Juvenile literature. | Emotions in adolescence—Juvenile
    literature.
Classification: LCC BF724.3.A55 T66 2020 | DDC 152.4/7—dc23
LC record available at https://lccn.loc.gov/2020013654

TABLE OF CONTENTS

NOTE TO THE READER   V

CHAPTER 1   Anger and You   1

CHAPTER 2   Record and Reflect   11

CHAPTER 3   Cool Your Angry Body   39

CHAPTER 4   Cool Your Angry Thoughts   53

CHAPTER 5   Stop the Drumbeat of Anger   89

CHAPTER 6   Communicate Clearly   113

CHAPTER 7   Solve Problems   137

CHAPTER 8   Handle Accusations and Put-Downs   147

CHAPTER 9   Build Self-Esteem and Self-Confidence   171

CHAPTER 10   Nutrition, Exercise, and Sleep   203

CHAPTER 11   Help, Hope, and Heads-Up   223

RESOURCES   255

INDEX   261

ACKNOWLEDGMENTS   279

ABOUT THE AUTHOR   280

NOTE TO THE READER

High-performance cars can go from zero to 60 in just a few seconds. That's moving; and that's what anger can feel like sometimes. One minute you're cool and calm and the next minute, in a flash, you're boiling. When that happens, people tell you to chill out or to calm down. They ask you, "Why are you so mean?" or "Why do you blow up all the time?" They tell you to cool down, but they don't tell you *how* to do it. Like you can turn off your anger like a light switch. They don't understand how difficult it is for you to calm down and that if you could, you would. The idea that you should know how to control your anger when no one has ever taught you how to do it is kind of ridiculous, right? That doesn't mean you can't learn. The tools in this book will help you.

Own Your Anger

Anger is an interesting emotion. People tend not to like anger. Anger can push people away or even frighten them. This makes it difficult for people to understand others who are angry, in the same way they understand people who are stressed, anxious, or depressed. When people are stressed, anxious, or depressed, others will often sympathize with them and tell them that it isn't their fault that they feel the way they do. When people are angry, however, the same doesn't apply. People often blame others for feeling and acting angry because they believe they could just calm down if they wanted to. This makes it hard for people to *own the anger* and ask for help. It's not easy to own a problem. It takes courage to stare down the anger and decide to take it on.

But you might see anger as something outside of your control and think you wouldn't be angry if people treated you differently. You might think if your teachers didn't load you with so much homework, or if your friends did things your way, or if people left you alone, then you wouldn't get angry. It's them, not you, and to a degree that's true. Other people do play a role. Sometimes people say something that hurts your feelings or treat you unfairly. Sometimes people do these things intentionally, and sometimes accidentally. What you have the most control over is how you react to these things. Owning your anger means you don't blame your friends, your school, your parents, or yourself. Owning your anger is the first step in taking charge of it.

Admit the Benefits of Anger and Give It Back

Have you ever lost your temper to get out of class, homework, or chores? Have you ever lost your temper so you could get your way? Have you ever lost your temper and put someone down so you could feel better about yourself? Part of owning your anger means admitting that sometimes you use anger to help you get want you want. But understanding the payoffs and realizing that you do this doesn't mean you don't want to overcome your anger. It just means you have two minds when it comes to working on it. One mind tells you that anger makes your life very hard. The other mind is comfortable with the way things are. If you think you benefit from getting angry sometimes, consider, at least for a while, seeing what you can accomplish without getting angry.

Otherwise, you may never know what you can do and what you can be.

Is This Book for You?

Think how different your life would be if you were able to keep your cool. What would change? Would you have more friends? Would more people invite you to hang out and do fun things? Would you feel less stressed at home and school? It's stressful to hold anger in and even more stressful to deal with the consequences when your anger pops out. Do you have a reputation you don't like? Do other people, even some of your close friends, see you as the kid with anger issues? Do teachers and coaches think you're touchy and sometimes lose their cool with you? If you want to change things, you can. You can control your anger, like many things in life, when you set aside some time to learn.

This book is for teens who want to learn tools to cool down, whether they're feeling anger, frustration, or irritation. The tools in this book are similar to those you might learn in cognitive-behavioral therapy (CBT), a type of psychotherapy that teaches people skills to manage problems such as anxiety, anger, and depression. Research shows that the CBT skills in this book can help you manage your anger and get back to enjoying your life.

How to Use This Book

Most people who struggle with anger believe they can't control it. They feel anger wash over them like a tsunami, suddenly, without warning, and there is nothing they can do to stop it. Perhaps that's what it feels like to you, too. Luckily, you *can* learn to control your anger with the tools in this book. We'll start with some basic information about the elements that drive anger: body, thoughts, and actions. Next, you'll learn tools to calm your body and mind. Tools you can tuck in your pocket to use the moment you feel the first signs of anger, like how to slow down the drumbeat of anger: that tendency to think and think and think about the injustice, hurt, and unfairness until you can't think of anything else. And skills to communicate with adults and peers effectively, so you can defuse situations that fuel anger. You'll learn how to solve problems quickly so that you don't feel stressed and frustrated, as well as how to de-escalate situations and respond to put-downs. Last, you'll learn skills to build your self-esteem and self-confidence. Strong self-esteem protects you from the anger that comes when you make a mistake, or disappoint friends, parents, or teachers. As you can see, it takes many tools to keep your cool. The material in this book is in an order so that one skill builds on another, but feel free to skip around.

I know what you're thinking: *More things to learn? Learning takes time. I do enough of that in school.* I've got great news: Learning skills to cool down doesn't take much time at all. Twenty minutes per day is probably all it takes. You can learn on the bus, before bed, or during lunch. Some of the skills in this book are ones that you likely already know and use, like counting to 10 or walking away. Once you learn one skill and see that it helps, you'll likely want to learn another. Learning is like that. You learn one thing and then you learn another; you make one change and then you make another. And then before you realize it—you've got it!

CHAPTER 1

Anger and You

Every teen—and every adult for that matter—feels angry from time to time, but zero-to-60 anger gets you into trouble. It can cause you to lose friends, hold you back in school or at work, and create more stress in your life. Zero-to-60 anger makes life hard, and it may feel like there's nothing you can do to stop the anger engine once it starts. The first step is to learn as much about anger as you can.

In this chapter, you'll learn about anger and what fuels it. You'll then hear from other teens who experience zero-to-60 anger. The stories they share throughout the book show what their anger felt like, how they worked through it, and how they developed a toolbox of cool-down skills to help them manage it.

What Is Anger?

Anger is a normal emotion, and it's there to protect you. Just like fear, anger tells you something is wrong. In other words, anger triggers your emergency alarm system. It's called the fight-or-flight response, and it's there to help you survive. When you sense danger, your mind and body catapult into action. Your mind releases hormones, and you get a burst of energy. Your heart starts to beat fast, and your blood pressure and breathing increase. Your face may flush as more blood flows to your arms and legs as your body prepares to act. Your attention narrows and locks intensely on what you perceive as the threat. Soon you can't pay attention to anything else. You're ready to fight.

Once your anger is turned on, it doesn't turn off quickly. The chemicals your brain released to turn on your anger remain in your system for a very long time. Your body might be tense and turned on for many hours—sometimes even days! This lingering physical tension lowers your anger threshold, making it easier for you to get very angry again in response to minor irritations that normally wouldn't bother you. This is the "just in case" part of your body's survival response; once your mind and body are amped and ready to fight, it's better to stay ready for a while, just in case you're threatened again.

This survival response is automatic and quick. In fact, it's so quick that it shoots right past the thinking part of your brain, particularly the part responsible for judgment. Because your brain is still a (relatively) young brain, things like judgment and anticipating consequences of actions don't come as easily to your brain as they do to an adult's brain. This doesn't mean that you're not smart; it just means your brain is a work in progress.

Anger Fuel

Anger isn't a mental health problem the way depression is a mental health problem. There are a million reasons you might get angry. If you're sad, you can feel irritable and get easily frustrated, which means that you might pop off from time to time. If you're scared because someone is threatening to hurt you, you might get angry so you can defend yourself. If you're stressed because you have too many things to do or are worried about falling behind in school, you might get angry over little things like someone asking you to do something for them. If you feel embarrassed after you tripped up the stairs in front of friends, you might get angry and kick the stairs. Anger is usually secondary to fear, sadness, shame, embarrassment, and hurt feelings. Often, anger is so strong and quick that it covers feelings that you didn't even know were there! Here are a few of the most common feelings that anger covers, as well as typical situations that trigger it.

Hurt

Hurt commonly fuels anger. Imagine you're hanging out at home in bare feet. Your mom walks in the door from work and comes to give you a hug. She steps on your foot with the heel of her shoe. You scream and then angrily push her away. First the hurt—ouch—and then the anger. There are tons of different hurts; physical and emotional. There can be hurt when a relationship you're in ends, when you lose a big game, or when you're teased by others. Whatever the cause, hurt can turn into zero-to-60 anger before you realize it.

I can't seem to stop fighting with everyone. My mom told me that I was just a kid, and that I would get over Jake. Obviously I was pissed about that. My friends were supportive at first, but now I can tell they're tired of hearing about it. It makes me so mad at them. They don't care about how I'm hurting—fine, then I won't care about their problems either. Dad tried to talk to me about it, and we've always been close, but I ended up screaming at him, too. I wish I could just stop feeling like this.

—Emma

Stress

Chronic stress is another fuel for anger. Stress makes your body tense and on edge. A tense body can cause you to feel irritable and impatient, which makes it easier for you to blow up. If you're stressed, you might have trouble tolerating the hundreds of little frustrations that arise every day: the school bus is late, your phone battery is low, your brother ate the last of the cereal. Normally, you'd shake off these little things, but when you're stressed, you might explode.

> I'm totally stressed, and I've started to lose it. Every time I turn around, someone wants me to do something. A friend asked me if I wanted to hang out after class. My dad asked if I would help put the dishes away. My math teacher asked me to tutor a couple of students. They don't get that I'm maxed out! I'm already barely sleeping, with all the work I'm doing studying and applying to colleges. When am I supposed to have time to tutor kids, too?? I got a C on a math quiz yesterday—I've never gotten a C on anything before. Then I screamed at Sean when he ate some of my fries at lunch. He always does that, but this time I just couldn't deal. Now my best friend isn't talking to me. I need to do something; I need to figure out how to get my anger under control.
>
> —Jamal

Shame

Shame is a powerful emotion. Guilt and shame are different, although they can sometimes feel the same. Guilt is when you feel bad about something you did. Shame is when you feel bad about *yourself* and not just about what you did. Shame sends powerful self-messages, such as, "I'm bad," "I'm disgusting," or "I'm unlovable." When an event triggers shame, you might strike back with anger to get away from the shame you're feeling. It's a bit like the magician who misdirects the audience's attention during a card trick. Anger diverts your attention away from the shame you feel.

> I've always had anger issues, but this year it's worse than ever. I thought high school would be different, but it's not. I'm such an idiot. The work is even harder, which makes my dyslexia even worse, and I'm falling behind faster than ever. Some of my teachers try to tell me I'm smart and that I would do well if I worked harder. They don't get it. No one does. My friends are all mad at me—it seems like every day I'm picking a fight with someone else. Before, everyone would just let it go and it would be no big deal, but now I've got a rep as "the angry guy," and I don't know how to patch things up when they all expect the worst from me. My friends were the only good thing about school—now it all sucks. I think I'll fake sick so I don't have to go tomorrow.
> —Jason

Depression

When you're depressed, you're often grouchy and irritable. You can be angry toward friends, family members, and yourself. When you're depressed, you might not even try to manage your anger. You don't see the point of holding back. You no longer care about friends. You no longer care about much of anything, so why care about the consequences of your anger on others and yourself?

" I hate my new school and I hate Mom for leaving Dad and making us come here. I've tried to make friends, but the girls here are horrible. Yesterday a girl got in my face and told me no one wanted me here and I should watch my back. I was so scared, I couldn't stop shaking. I tried to just ignore it, but when I got home I lost it and exploded at my mom. I screamed and threw a magazine at her. But it's all her fault I'm here anyway! And today, I went off on everyone, even the few girls who were nice to me. I even yelled at Mr. Shannon, who is my favorite teacher. He told me that I have to stop exploding at everyone, but I don't know how to stop. I feel so alone, sad, and angry all the time, and it just makes me want to fight. I need to get it under control.
—Camila **"**

Family

You've likely learned a few things from your family over the years. You've learned how to wash dishes, how to change a tire, and how to handle anger. You might have learned that anger is normal, or that no one will listen to you until you get angry, or to hold emotions in until they burst out in a flood of anger. Although you can't change your family, understanding how your family handles anger can help you understand why and how you handle it.

> 66
> It's gotten bad between me and my mom. She's treating me like a kid, and it's driving me crazy. She doesn't trust me and asks me a million questions every time I go out. Or she tells me I can go out but then changes her mind. I'm almost an adult, but she doesn't seem to get that. I get so angry every time she asks me a question, which just makes it worse. She starts to freak out, and then I start to freak out, and it usually ends with me running to my room and slamming the door. What makes it worse is that I know I'm doing the same thing my dad did. I see it happening, but I don't know how to stop.
> —Ayanna
> 99

Self-Esteem

Self-esteem is how much you like and appreciate yourself. If your self-esteem is low, you might not like yourself. You might believe you're worthless, meaningless, and a failure. You might believe you're ugly or stupid. You might even hate yourself because you can't handle the anger. When your self-esteem is weak or fragile, it's easily bruised. This means that even little things, like failing a quiz, going through a breakup, or stumbling in front of friends, can hurt horribly. Reacting with anger seems like the only way to cover how badly you feel about yourself.

66 Coach came by my house today. At first I didn't even want to talk to him—it's his fault I'm suspended, he kicked me off the team! But my mom made me sit down with him. He told me I'm a great soccer player (I already know that!) and the only thing between me and playing is my anger. He tried to blame my grades on my anger too—I told him it's not MY fault, the teachers all hate me, and the principal is a jerk, and I don't need math to play soccer anyway. Then he said that if I want to play soccer in college, I have

to have the grades to get there, and that a cool head is just as important as fancy footwork. No team wants the player who's always causing locker room drama. I'm still not convinced about math, but I know he's right about learning to keep my cool.

—Alejandro **99**

IN A *NUTSHELL*

Anger is a normal emotion, except when it's not. Zero-to-60 anger is too quick and too fast, and most teens have a hard time managing it. It may feel like the anger is in charge of you and your life.

1. Anger is a normal emotion, and just like fear, it's there to protect you. It tells you that something is wrong and motivates you to fix it.

2. Every teen feels angry from time to time and for different reasons. Hurt, stress, shame, and sadness, as well as fragile self-esteem, are just a few of the things that fuel zero-to-60 anger.

The only difference between the usual anger and zero-to-60 anger is how you handle it, and it's not your fault that you don't know how yet. You don't have the tools right now. But when you do, you'll be able to cool down.

CHAPTER 2

Record and Reflect

Zero-to-60 anger can feel like it hits suddenly and without warning, but anger doesn't really work that way. It sends early warning signs, and if you understand your anger signals, you can get ahead of it a little. Keeping a record of your anger outbursts is the first step to understanding and, eventually, controlling them. Once you start keeping track of your anger outbursts, you can then reflect on the typical ways you think and act that fuel your anger. Reflecting also includes accepting the minuses and understanding the pluses of anger so that you can decide whether anger truly works for you or you work for it. That's why this chapter is so important. It may be the most important chapter in the book. If you don't understand your anger, then you won't know when to use the tools to slow it down, which tools to use, and why you would even want to try.

ABCs of Anger

The ABCs of Anger include Antecedents, Basics, and Consequences. Look at Jason's ABCs of Anger form on the next page as you learn more about the parts of your anger outbursts.

JASON'S ABCs OF ANGER

Antecedent — A kid bumps into me in the cafeteria and I drop my tray of food.

Basics of Anger

Angry Body — Clench my teeth. My face feels hot. I'm squinting at him.

Angry Thoughts — He did that on purpose!

Angry Actions — I get in the kid's face and kick the food that's on the floor onto his shoes.

Consequences — A teacher comes over, yells at me, and tells me to leave the cafeteria. I miss lunch and I'm hungry all day.

Antecedents of Anger

Antecedents are the people and events that trigger anger. The Antecedents of Anger differ from person to person, depending on who they are and their circumstances. For example, a friend who shares something private about you with another person might trigger your anger, but this same situation might not bother someone else. Memories or thinking about the past can trigger anger, too. It's important to know your triggers.

TYPICAL ANGER ANTECEDENTS

Instructions: Look at the list of typical Anger Antecedents for teens and notice the ones that rev your anger engine. You probably have some that aren't on the list, too!

Touching your things without your permission.	Bossing you around.
Gossiping about you.	Nagging you.
Sharing personal information about you to other people.	Accusing you of doing something you didn't do.
Teasing you.	Borrowing something of yours without your permission.
Getting into your face or space.	Making annoying sounds.
Breaking or losing your things.	Accusing you of saying something you didn't say.
Sharing your texts without your permission.	Wearing or using your things without your permission.

Basics of Anger

The Basics of Anger are: angry body, angry thoughts, and angry actions. These basics are the gears of the anger engine. These gears work together to increase your anger and keep it going. You'll learn tools later that target these basics and help you slow the anger engine.

Angry Body. These are the physical signs of anger. Your heart beats faster, your breathing quickens, and your jaw or fists tighten: you're ready to act. As your anger builds, your body is primed and ready to go from zero to 60. Also, these intense physical signs of anger linger long after the initial anger rush has passed. This means your angry body is primed and ready to shoot from zero to 60 again, and quickly, over minor things. When you record an anger outburst, you'll write these physical signs of your anger in the Angry Body column in the ABCs of Anger form.

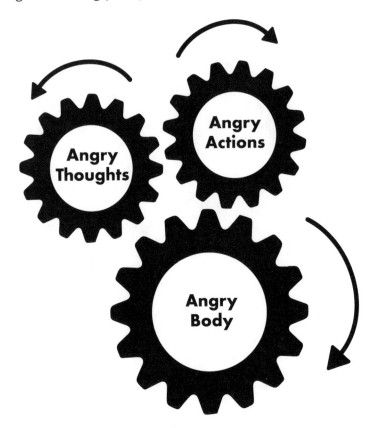

Angry Thoughts. Usually, you're more aware of your angry body than your angry thoughts. That's okay, but your angry thoughts can make a big difference in how often and how intensely you're angry. Angry thoughts of all kinds—assumptions, predictions, and conclusions—affect how you read a situation and how you resolve conflicts. For example, the most common thought an angry mind generates is that people intentionally do things to make you angry. Also, pictures or images that run through your mind can fuel your anger, too, such as the image of hitting another kid, or screaming at your parents. Or, an urge might run through your mind, "I'm gonna punch that kid." When you record an anger outburst, you'll write these thoughts, images, and urges in the Angry Thoughts column in the ABCs of Anger form.

Angry Actions. Now for the real troublemaker: angry actions. The problem with zero-to-60 anger isn't about feeling angry. The problem is how you handle the anger you feel. There are two types of angry actions: physical actions and mental actions. Physical actions, like screaming at a friend when she interrupts you, or flipping off your teacher when he asks you to stay after class, is all about acting before thinking.

There's another angry action that might seem like an angry thought, but it's not. It's a thought *action*: thinking and re-thinking about an anger-provoking event or situation. This is the drumbeat of anger or anger rumination. Anger rumination thoughts aren't the thoughts that make you angry but they're the thoughts that *keep* you angry. The drumbeat of anger is your mind thinking over and over, around and around, about the past hurt, slight, or unfairness. Acting without thinking can cause problems, but thinking too much about anger-provoking events can cause problems, too. Anger rumination intensifies your anger which then increases the likelihood that you'll act in an angry way. Anger rumination can interfere with good listening, too. It's like you're singing one song while trying to listen to another one. If you can't listen, then you're more likely to misunderstand what the other person is saying. Poor listening leads to conflict and more problems for you. Last, it's difficult to concentrate on your homework or soccer practice when the drum of anger is beating. When you record an anger outburst, you'll write the thoughts that go around and around in your mind in the Angry Actions column in the ABCs of Anger form.

Consequences of Anger

Things that happen to you—the really unpleasant things—after an anger outburst are Consequences. Like when a teacher yells at you, or you're grounded for the weekend, or you lose another friend. It's important to understand the consequences that follow an anger outburst. Understanding and remembering the consequences of anger will motivate you to continue the difficult work of learning and practicing the tools to help cool your anger.

You'll learn about the consequences of anger later in this chapter. For now, pay attention to what happens after an anger outburst. Usually, this means paying attention to what happens after an angry action. For example, you yell at your mom (Angry Action) and you lose screen time for the day (Consequence). When you record an anger outburst, you'll write the consequences you experienced in the Consequence column on the ABCs of Anger form. Try to describe exactly what happened rather than your opinions of what happened. For example, write, "My teacher sent me to the principal's office," rather than, "I didn't do anything wrong, but my teacher sent me to the principal's office anyway." Or, write "Bethany didn't talk to me for the rest of the week," rather than, "Bethany thinks she's too good to talk to me."

Make several copies of the blank ABCs of Anger form (on the next page) and record your anger outbursts over the next few days. Understanding the ABCs of Anger as well as recording how they come up in your life is an important tool. If you don't know the ABCs of your anger, it's nearly impossible to tap the breaks when the anger engine is revving.

ABCs OF ANGER

ntecedent ....

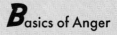**asics of Anger**

            Angry Body ....

                                    ....

       Angry Thoughts ....

                                    ....

       Angry Actions ....

                                    ....

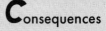**onsequences** ....

                                    ....

> 66 Wow. Back to preschool for me, but just learning the ABCs of anger helped me feel a little more in control of my anger engine. When I started keeping track, I realized that the same thing tends to trigger my anger. It's when someone asks me to do something when I'm already feeling super stressed. I also noticed that I tend to have the same angry thoughts—usually that people don't know or care how stressed I am. It was hard to face the consequences of my out-of-control anger engine though. I don't like to think about those, even though I know that they're there. I keep telling myself that the anger isn't a big deal and that I can control it. But deep down, I know it's making my life really hard.
> —Jamal 99

Anger ABC Cycle

If anger just happened randomly without any pattern, there wouldn't be much you could do to stop it. Although it may feel like every anger outburst is different, every occurrence covers the same ground: antecedent (trigger), anger basics, and consequences. Understanding your anger cycle can help you slow your anger because you'll know what to expect. Jason reviewed several of his ABCs of Anger forms when he blew up at his dad. Jason discovered his anger outbursts with his dad typically covered the same ground, over and over.

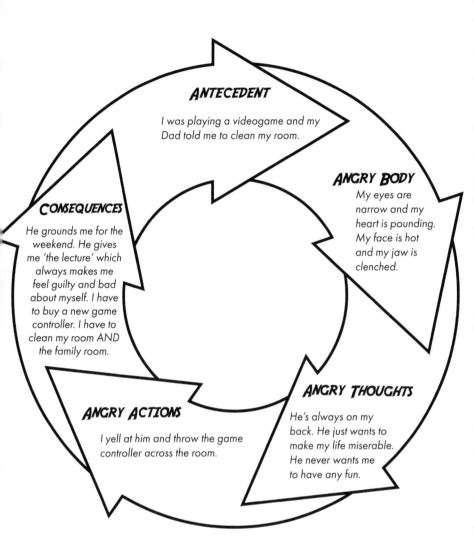

ANTECEDENT

I was playing a videogame and my Dad told me to clean my room.

ANGRY BODY

My eyes are narrow and my heart is pounding. My face is hot and my jaw is clenched.

ANGRY THOUGHTS

He's always on my back. He just wants to make my life miserable. He never wants me to have any fun.

ANGRY ACTIONS

I yell at him and throw the game controller across the room.

CONSEQUENCES

He grounds me for the weekend. He gives me 'the lecture' which always makes me feel guilty and bad about myself. I have to buy a new game controller. I have to clean my room AND the family room.

Your Body's Anger Signals

Your body and mind send anger signals long before you become aware of them. In order to learn to cool down, it's important you know these signals. Noticing the first signs of anger when it's low—when you're just irritated rather than boiling—will help you catch the anger early so you can use the tools in this book.

> It surprised me to learn that my anger follows pretty much the same pattern almost all the time. My dad wants me to do well in school. I get that, but he's always on me about my schoolwork! When he asks about school or reminds me to do my homework, I blow up and yell at him. Then he takes away something, and lectures me. I always feel terrible after he tells me that he's disappointed, that we should be able to work things out calmly rather than always having a big fight. Then it's like all this is my fault, and it makes me even angrier. I  keep repeating the same pattern, feeling and thinking the same things and running into the same consequences. At least now I know that pretty much any time my dad asks about school, I'll probably blow up. Knowing that has helped a little.
>
> —Jason

Scan Your Body and Mind for Anger

By this time, you've probably completed several ABCs of Anger forms and have identified your angry body and mind signals. For example, your angry body signals might include clenching your jaw or your heart pounding. Angry mind signals might include thoughts such as "I hate you," "Shut up," or "I'm going to hit you." Another way to get to know your anger signals is to scan your mind and body for these first signs of anger. In the following exercise, you'll think back to an old grudge or even a recent situation that triggered an anger outburst. You'll then slowly scan your body for any tension, tightness, or other sensations that signal anger, and scan your mind for anger thoughts. Remember, anger thoughts are automatic and tend to run below the radar. You're likely less aware of the anger thoughts than the signals of an angry body because you haven't learned to pay attention. This activity will help you notice your angry thoughts and angry body signals.

The goal of this exercise is to become aware of the signals your body and mind send when you feel angry. Try noticing what you feel and think. Do you notice that your jaw is tight or that your face is hot? What thoughts or pictures are going through your mind? Your mind will inevitably wander away from time to time, which is natural and happens to everyone. When you notice your mind has wandered, gently acknowledge it, and then return your attention to the part of the body on which you're focusing. Read and record the following body and mind scan script and then listen to the recording to do the exercise. If you've never done a body scan or meditation before, it's going to seem a little repetitive at first—it's supposed to be like that! When you record the script, try to read it slowly and clearly, with pauses between the steps, so you can follow along later without feeling rushed. The repetition really helps you to focus in the moment when you do the scan.

> **STEP 1:** Lie down in a comfortable place like a carpeted floor, couch or bed. Gently close your eyes. Although you may feel sleepy during this exercise, try to remain awake and aware of your body in the present moment.

STEP 2: Think back to a grudge or situation when you felt angry. Allow yourself to think and feel the anger again. Allow the anger to return as you remember the event that made you angry.

STEP 3: Now, bring your awareness to your left foot. Scan your left foot for any sensations. Start at your toes, and move your awareness slowly through your sole, heel, and ankle. Notice if you have any tension or discomfort in any part of your foot. Now, gently tune in to your thoughts. Notice any images. Notice all thoughts that flow through your mind while you remember the grudge. Notice and remember these sensations and thoughts. Notice your breath, without trying to change it.

STEP 4: Now slowly scan up your left calf. Notice and allow any sensations that may be present. Scan slowly, up through your thigh now. Allow yourself to feel any and all sensations. If you don't feel anything at the moment, that's okay. Just allow yourself to notice what you don't feel. Slowly become aware of your thoughts again. Notice any images. Notice all thoughts that flow through your mind while you remember the grudge. Notice and remember these sensations and thoughts. If you notice angry thoughts, acknowledge them: "I hear you. I see you. But I'm busy right now." Let the thoughts go, and re-focus on your body. If it's hard to let the thoughts go, that's okay; try to just bring your attention to your breath and the physical sensations in your body.

STEP 5: When you become aware of any tension or discomfort in a particular part of your body, notice and acknowledge it, and then breathe into the sensation to bring a gentle awareness to it, without trying to change it. Become aware of your thoughts again. Notice all thoughts and images that flow through your mind while you remember the grudge. Notice and remember these sensations and thoughts. Acknowledge and release them.

STEP 6: Now scan for any sensations in your right foot, calf, and thigh. Simply notice all sensations and feel what is happening. Continue to bring awareness and a gentle curiosity to the sensations in your right leg. Slowly become aware of your thoughts. Continue to notice, acknowledge, and release any anger thoughts as you remember the grudge. Re-focus on your breath and the physical sensations in your body.

STEP 7: Now focus on your stomach. Feel it rising as you breathe in. Sinking as you exhale. Nice and slow. Your heart rate may slow as you relax more and more. This is normal. Remain aware of your stomach and notice any sensations in your stomach area. Bring a gentle awareness to any tightness or discomfort in your stomach, and notice and remember any sensations there. Now, slowly become aware of your thoughts. Notice all thoughts that flow through your mind while you remember the grudge. Acknowledge and release them.

STEP 8: Now scan for any sensations in your left hand and arm. Simply become aware of the different sensations and feel what is happening. Continue to bring awareness and a gentle curiosity to the sensations. Again, if you don't feel anything at the moment, that's okay. Slowly become aware of your thoughts now. Notice all thoughts and images that flow through your mind while you remember the grudge. Notice and remember these sensations and thoughts, without judging them. Release them and re-focus on your breath and body.

STEP 9: Scan for sensations in your right hand and arm. Continue to bring awareness and a gentle curiosity to the sensations. Start at the very tips of your fingers, and travel slowly up through you palm, your wrist, your forearm, your elbow, and all the way up to your shoulder. Breathe into any areas of discomfort or tension. Slowly become aware of your thoughts. Notice any images. Notice all thoughts that flow through your mind while you remember the grudge. Notice and remember these sensations and thoughts. Acknowledge them and refocus on your body.

STEP 10: Come back to your chest. Continue scanning up and along your neck, and to your face. Feel the sensations in your jaw, and in your throat. Notice how the back of your head rests against the surface under you. Bring your awareness to the top of your head. Notice and remember any sensations there or in your jaw, neck, or throat. Slowly, as before, become aware of your thoughts as you remember the grudge. Notice all thoughts that flow through your mind and remember these sensations and thoughts. Notice if there are any changes in the way your face and neck feel. Acknowledge and release any thoughts and changes.

STEP 11: Now take a moment to notice how all your body parts are feeling. Let any sensations come to you. Just notice the sensation—warm, tingling, tight, heavy. Accept the sensation as it is. It is a sensation in this part of your body. Bring your awareness to your full body. Slowly become aware of all your thoughts. Accept these thoughts as you become aware of your body and mind in this moment. Notice all thoughts that flow through your mind while you remember the grudge. Notice and remember any sensations in your body and thoughts in your mind during this exercise.

STEP 12: Continue to focus on your breathing as long as you like, noticing and remembering any sensations, and noticing and remembering any thoughts during this exercise.

Now that you've completed the body scan, look at the list of typical body and mind anger signals below and make a note of each one—even if it wasn't intense—you noticed during the body scan exercise you just tried.

BODY AND MIND ANGER SIGNALS

Body	Mind
Feeling like your face and neck are hot.	"I hate you."
Grinding your teeth.	"Shut up."
Breathing heavily.	"I want to hit you."
Trembling.	"Don't mess with me."
Hands and arms are tense.	"Back off."
Grimacing.	"You did it on purpose."
Corners of mouth are turned down.	"That's not fair."
Sweating.	"I can't believe you did that."
Neck and shoulders are tense and tight.	"I didn't do it."
Feeling nauseated.	"Get away from me."
Head throbbing.	"You don't care about me."
Crying.	"I'll show you."
Looking down.	"You're not listening to me."
Breathing heavily.	"You always do that."
Feeling lightheaded or dizzy.	"It's all your fault."

> I've learned that knowing my body and mind anger signals helps me get ahead of the anger a little. I never knew when anger was building because I wasn't paying attention. I just exploded. Now that I know my body and mind anger signals, I can do a little something that helps. Like the other day, my mom asked me to help her with some things for my school's fundraiser next month. I started to feel my jaw tighten. That's one of my body's anger signals. I noticed that I was thinking, "She doesn't care how stressed I am," which is an angry mind thought I have sometimes. I decided to tell her that I was feeling pretty stressed with a college application that was due in two weeks. She thanked me for letting her know and then let me off the hook. I didn't need to explode.
>
> —Jamal

Your Anger Thermometer

Now that you know where in your body anger simmers, the next step is to learn to rate the level of anger. This may seem silly, but it's an important tool for handling anger. Knowing your anger level can help you decide when and how to respond. For example, if your anger is high, it is often better to walk away or use the calm body tools you'll learn in the next chapter. Staying in the situation when your anger is high is a formula for a consequence, and perhaps a big one.

Look at Jason's anger thermometer. He used the ABC records he completed to create his anger thermometer. It was all there. His body and mind signals were in the Basics of Anger columns. He also looked over what he wrote after he completed his body and mind scan. He had listed a few body and mind anger signals that he hadn't remembered for his ABC records. He then placed the body and mind signals at different anger temperature levels: enraged, angry, irritated, and annoyed. Jason might update his anger thermometer as he learns more about his body and mind anger signals.

Now, complete your own anger thermometer. Take a look at the ABCs of Anger records you've completed. What body and mind anger signals do you have? Perhaps you'll see an anger signal clue or two from the body and mind scan you completed.

JASON'S ANGER THERMOMETER		
Temperature	Angry Body Signals	Angry Mind Signals
Enraged (100)	Yelling Jaw clenched Body shaking	"I hate you." "I want to hit you."
Angry (75)	Heart racing Face flushed Voice trembling	"Back off." "You're an idiot."
Irritated (50)	Looking down Jaw clenched Frowning	"Get away from me." "You're annoying."
Annoyed (25)	Chest tight Squinting Restless	"Leave me alone." "Shut up."

Place these signals next to the level of anger you think you feel. It's okay to guess. If it's hard to assign a temperature number, just put the signals next to a color. For example, enraged might be red while annoyed might be yellow.

MY ANGER THERMOMETER

Temperature	Angry Body Signals	Angry Mind Signals
Enraged (100)	_____	_____
	_____	_____
	_____	_____
Angry (75)	_____	_____
	_____	_____
	_____	_____
Irritated (50)	_____	_____
	_____	_____
	_____	_____
Annoyed (25)	_____	_____
	_____	_____
	_____	_____

Pluses and Minuses of Anger

There are pluses and minuses for everything you do. If you do something fun rather than study: your enjoyment in the moment is a plus. But if you then fail the test because you didn't study: that's a minus. If you take the shot and sink it rather than pass the ball to a teammate who's closer to the hoop: that's a plus because you made the shot. If you miss the shot, however, your teammate and coach are upset with you for not passing; that's a minus. Anger, particularly angry actions, has pluses and minuses too.

Minuses of Anger

Even though anger signals there's a problem, angry actions don't always solve the problem. Angry actions—when it's zero-to-60 anger—create more problems for you. Angry actions just keep anger going because stress primes anger, and nothing is more stressful than dealing with the consequences of out-of-control anger. In many of the chapters that follow, you'll learn tools to resist angry actions. Here's a list of the typical Anger Minuses that teens with zero-to-60 anger experience. As you read through these sections, refer back to this list of Anger Minuses. Write down problems you've experienced in each of these categories as you go.

Friends. Zero-to-60 anger can cost you friends. Maybe in the past, a friend has said things like: "I don't like people screaming at me," or, "Hey, chill out." You might think the friend deserves your anger, and perhaps they do, but that's one fewer friend in your life. Good friends may take it once, perhaps even two or three times, but sooner or later, they give up on you. Have you lost a significant other because they're fed up with the anger? If you still have a significant other, do you fight a lot over the same things? It's hard to be around someone whose anger is quick and unpredictable. Zero-to-60 anger makes for lonely days. Eating alone at lunch. Sitting alone in your room. Walking from one class to the next alone. After a while, zero-to-60 anger is the only company you have, or perhaps you've found new friends, but they have zero-to-60 anger too. Perhaps these new friends aren't your first choice as friends, but at least you have friends to hang out with.

Money. Zero-to-60 anger is expensive. Yes, it feels good to blow off steam for a couple of seconds, but then the bills start coming in. There is the phone you threw against the wall. The window you broke when you slammed the door. The textbook you threw out the car window, or the necklace you ripped from your neck. Anger is expensive, and anger isn't going to pay the bill.

Family. Zero-to-60 anger is hard on you and your family. Your parents are exhausted by the anger and have tried everything to solve the anger problem. They've grounded you. They've talked to you. They've tried ignoring the anger, and perhaps they've become angry themselves. Your brothers and sisters might walk away from you at school because they worry that one of your anger outbursts will embarrass them again.

School and work. Zero-to-60 anger makes it nearly impossible to succeed in school. Teachers may have given you one warning and then another, and still the anger keeps coming. Other students might feel frustrated with you because they just want to get through class rather than waiting again for the teacher to deal with your anger.

You may have lost one job after another. No employer will write you a letter of reference and you wouldn't ask for one. Teachers, principals, employers, other students, and co-workers are tired of being the target of anger and the target of blame. Most importantly, think about the opportunities you've lost: to learn, to have fun, and to have new and exciting experiences.

Stress, worry, embarrassment, and guilt. Zero-to-60 anger is stressful. It takes a lot of energy and effort to manage your life when anger is creating so many problems for you. You may not sleep well because you're stressed or because the drumbeat of anger keeps you awake. Then there's the worry about the consequences of anger. Will your parents ground you again? Will the principal expel you? Perhaps you called a friend a name, and you wish you could take it back. That's embarrassing. Perhaps you acted like a jerk when you lost it. That's embarrassing too. You might wish you could take it all back and promise to others and yourself you won't blow up again. You feel guilty and bad.

Self-image. Zero-to-60 anger can change you. Friends might talk amongst themselves and say you're nice sometimes but you have an anger problem. You start to get a reputation, and that follows you wherever you go. Zero-to-60 anger gets in the way of being who you truly are: honest, fair, caring, and kind. You have an image problem and, deep down, you're trapped in an image that isn't you, but you don't know how to change it.

Pluses of Anger

The minuses of zero-to-60 anger are pretty obvious, even though it may be difficult to admit that you have them sometimes. The pluses of anger can be less obvious, but they're there. To truly solve the zero-to-60 anger problem, it's important to identify and then decide to set aside the pluses. Often, the pluses of anger help you in the moment. The minuses come later—sometimes much later—and can change the course of your life, such as graduating from college or getting a good job. Look at the list of Anger Pluses and note the ones that fit for you. Be as honest with yourself as you can.

- Gets me away from feelings like hurt, embarrassment, fear.
- Gets me what I want from friends or family members.
- Gets me away from people who scare me.
- Gets me out of doing homework.
- Gets me out of jobs I don't want to do.
- Gets me out of doing something new and stressful.
- Gets me out of doing something that's boring.
- Gets me attention when I want it.
- Gets me out of doing something that might embarrass me.
- Gets me power when I feel powerless.
- Gets me revenge on people I don't like.
- Gets me friends to hang out with.
- Gets me money or other things I want or like.

Let Your Values Lead the Way

Slowing and stopping anger isn't easy. It may be one of the most difficult things you've ever tried to do. You've likely been thinking the same things and doing the same things over and over for so long that anger has become a habit. Changing a habit isn't easy. It takes work and, most importantly, a willingness to make difficult changes in the way you've been doing things. Believe it or not, changing these anger habits will do more than just help you manage your anger. Changing these habits will bring out the best parts of yourself. These parts are the core of who you are. These are your core values. Taking time to identify your core values will help you stay on track as you begin to change your deeply ingrained anger habits.

So, what's a core value? There's the last scene of "The Wizard of Oz" in which Dorothy and her friends, Lion, Scarecrow, and Tin Man stand next to her. As they say goodbye to each other, the wizard honors their unique core values. For the Lion, it is courage. For the Scarecrow, it is intelligence. For the Tin Man, it is love. And for Dorothy, it is family or home. Imagine that you're standing there too. What would your core values be? Is friendship one of your core values? If yes, this might explain how much time and effort you're willing to put into making your friendships caring and supportive. Is creativity one of your core values? If yes, this might explain your passion for drawing or music. Is it achievement? If yes, this might explain your willingness to practice your free throw shots over and over. Core values are the personal beliefs and principles that guide how you wish to live your life, what you wish to stand for, and who you wish to be. Core values are the internal compass that guides you in the right direction. In the table below, note the five core values that are most important to you. Feel free to add other core values to the list.

MY CORE VALUES

Values About Family and Friends

Dependability.

Loyalty.

Honesty.

Helpfulness.

Harmony.

Fun.

_____

_____

Values About School/Sports/Work

Achievement.

Excellence.

Teamwork.

Leadership.

Knowledge.

Curiosity.

_____

_____

Values About Play and Creativity

Imagination.

Uniqueness.

Freedom.

Innovation.

Harmony.

Worldly beauty.

_____

_____

Values About Health and Wellbeing

Self-improvement.

Calmness.

Endurance.

Fitness.

Self-reliance.

Self-care.

_____

_____

> Last weekend my dad and I were together for our annual daughter-dad camping trip. We were headed back to camp after a hike across Bear Valley. The valley is beautiful with mountains on each side: Big Bear and Little Bear mountains. My dad told me to keep my eye on this one rock formation on Little Bear Mountain; our camp was right under it, so it was easy to navigate back if we could see it. Once, my dad headed in the wrong direction, and I noticed before he did that we were off course. That rock formation is kind of like a core value—something to guide me to where I want to go. I'll probably get off track a few times as I learn to slow the anger engine, but if I let my core values lead the way, I'll get back on track pretty quickly.
>
> —Camila

IN A NUTSHELL

Reflecting and recording are important tools in handling your anger. You can learn the best anger management tools in the world, but they're useless to you if you don't know when to use them. Reflecting also includes accepting the minuses and understanding the pluses of anger so you can decide whether anger truly works for you or you work for it.

1. The ABCs of Anger, particularly the Anger Basics (angry body, angry mind, angry actions) together drive the anger engine. Understanding these and how they work together and fuel your anger is essential in order to learn when and how to apply the tools in this book.

2. Remember your body and mind anger signals. Knowing these signals decreases the likelihood that the anger engine revs up out of your control. Also, knowing your anger signals helps you decide which tools to use and when.

3. Every action creates minuses and pluses for you. Knowing the minuses can help motivate you to learn and practice the tools in this book. Knowing the pluses, and accepting you have them, will help you make the slow but important changes in how you choose to live your life.

CHAPTER 3

Cool Your Angry Body

It's often easier to start a car when the engine is warm than when it's cold. A warm engine turns over easily; so easily that the car can go from zero to 60 in seconds. It's screaming down the road in a blink. A cold engine, on the other hand, is sluggish. Although it can get to 60, it takes time. Anger is like that too. If you're warm—that is, if you're tense, or stressed, or on edge— your anger can have you in the fast lane before you can blink. Stress and tension can fuel anger. Learning to calm your body is an important step in keeping your cool.

In this chapter, you'll learn five important calm body tools:

- Slow deep breathing
- Progressive muscle relaxation
- Positive imagery
- Counting to 10
- STOP

These tools are easy to learn and practice, and many people already use them to relax and calm down. Once you can relax your body, you can then learn to shift into automatic relaxation, which can help you cool down quickly. But it's best to practice these when you're already calm—it's almost impossible to learn something new when your anger engine is already in full throttle! Also, practicing relaxation tools every day helps keep your anger level low so you begin each day with less tension and less frustration.

Getting Started

Learning the breathing and relaxation tools takes a little preparation. Follow these steps to get the most out of every practice:

- Find a quiet place you can use for 10-15 minutes. Make sure there are no loud noises and no one will interrupt you.
- Set aside time every day to practice. Select a time that works best for you and start with 5 minutes each day. Increase by a couple of minutes every week until you're practicing 10 or 15 minutes per day.
- Make practice a priority. It'll be easier to commit to practicing each day if you believe it's important.

Now, you might be saying, "Yeah right, like I have time to do this." But it's only for a few minutes. Think for a minute—is there a time when things are less hectic for you, or when you can take a short break? This might be right after school before you start homework, or first thing on a Saturday or Sunday morning, or right before dinner. Also, remind yourself of the reasons you want to practice tools to cool down. Remember your list of minuses? Life is hard enough. Who needs the stress of dealing with the minuses of anger too?

> My coach told me that he meditates and it's super helpful and it's not just for people who do yoga to get all zen and chill. A bunch of his soccer buddies meditate, too. He says he uses it to just step back from the stress of the day for a moment. He showed me a meditation app with breathing and relaxation exercises that I could use, which would definitely make it easier. Some are only a couple of minutes long, so I'm going to give one of those a try and see if it works for me.
>
> —Alejandro

Breathe Slowly and Deeply

Slow deep breathing is the first Calm Body tool you'll learn. To practice slow deep breathing, get comfortable in a favorite chair or lie on your bed, uncross your legs and arms, and close your eyes.

1. Place one hand on your upper chest and the other hand just below your ribcage. This allows you to feel your diaphragm move as you breathe in and out.

2. Breathe in slowly through your nose so that your stomach moves out against your hand. Imagine your breath is going all the way down into your stomach and filling it up. Say the word "COOL" to yourself as you breathe in

slowly to the count of three. Imagine the word as you slowly inhale. Keep your hand on your chest as still as possible.

3. Hold your breath now as you again count one-two-three slowly in your head.

4. Next, say the word "CALM" to yourself and imagine the word in your mind's eye as you exhale through pursed lips to the count of three.

5. As you breathe, imagine the air traveling in and out of your lungs *slowly* and *evenly*. Take another slow, deep breath in through your nose as you count to three. Hold it for three seconds and release for three seconds. Pause for a moment, then again: inhale for three seconds. Hold for three and exhale for three. Pause.

Repeat this slow, deep, and rhythmic flow for a total of 10-15 minutes. If your mind wanders during the exercise, just refocus your attention on the picture of the word ("COOL" or "CALM") in your mind's eye and continue breathing in and out, noticing your chest rise and fall.

Relax Your Body

A stressed body sets the stage for anger, and most people—especially teens!—feel stressed a lot. Think of yourself as a balloon that fills with stress throughout the day. There are tests, homework, parties, sports competitions, friends, family, and a million other things. By the end of the day, you may feel like you're about to pop from so much stress, and perhaps sometimes you do. That's because you did not do anything to release stress from the balloon. The balloon just kept filling and filling until it couldn't fill any more. Learning to relax your muscles is a great tool to release the stress from the balloon, but it's important to do it every day. It's a like an antidote for stress. You do it every day so you start each new day with an empty stress balloon. The less stress you feel, the less likely you are to shoot from zero to 60.

Progressive muscle relaxation helps release pent up tension. Concert violinists repeatedly open and close their hands to relax them before they play. Professional basketball players shrug their shoulders or shake their heads before they take a free throw. These simple gestures release pent up tension, which helps muscles perform optimally. Just like famous musicians and athletes, you can learn to relax your muscles and decrease unwanted tension that can set you up to lose your cool. *Don't engage in this exercise if you have a medical condition that makes it unsafe for you to tense and relax your muscles.*

Begin by sitting or lying down with your arms by your side and your legs uncrossed out in front of you. Close your eyes.

1. Start by squeezing your eyes tight, scrunch your nose, pull the edges of your mouth back toward your ears into a forced smile, and bite down to tense your mouth and jaw. Hold this position for 15 seconds. Then, slowly release your eyes, nose, mouth, and jaw. Relax your face so all the wrinkles disappear, your face is smooth and relaxed, your cheeks feel soft, and your tongue is loose in your mouth. Keep your face relaxed like this for another 15 seconds. Notice how different this feels from when your face was tight and tense. Your muscles cannot hold a tense, tight position for very long, and it's important for you to learn to feel the difference between tension and relaxation so you can make your muscles relax when you notice they're tense.

2. Now, move to your neck and shoulders. Drop your chin to your chest and pull your shoulders up to your ears. Hold this position for 15 seconds, observing the tension in your neck and shoulder muscles. Now release, let your shoulders drop down, and relax your head. Hold this relaxed pose for 15 seconds.

3. Next, move on to the hands and arms. Make fists with your hands and cross your arms at the wrists. Hold your arms up in front of you and push them together as if you're arm wrestling with yourself. Hold your arms in this position with your fists clenched for 15 seconds. Then let your fists uncurl and your arms slowly fall to your sides. Hold this relaxed position for 15 seconds. Observe how your arms are feeling loose and heavy, and how this feeling of relaxation feels much better than when your muscles were tense and tight.

4. Next, suck in your stomach, making your abdomen get hard and tight, and clench your buttock muscles together. Hold this position for 15 seconds. Notice how the tension feels uncomfortable. Then release and let your stomach go out further and further while you release your buttock muscles. Relax like this for 15 seconds.

5. Last, stick your legs straight out in front of you and point your feet toward your head while you scrunch your toes into a tight ball. Hold for 15 seconds, then release and relax your feet and legs for 15 seconds. Your legs might feel loose and floppy as they begin to lose their tension.

You might notice as you go through all these muscle exercises, tensing and relaxing, that you're starting to feel more clam. You feel grounded as if you're melting into the floor. Your muscles might feel heavy and loose, and your whole body is beginning to feel relaxed. You're in charge of how your body feels, and you're commanding your muscles to relax.

You can repeat these six steps to relax your body even more, beginning again with your eyes closed.

Find Your Inner Calm Place

Imagining a peaceful, calm place is a great Calm Body tool and can be fun, too. Not only can imagining relax your body, it can relax your mind. Imagery is something you can do when you can't practice deep slow breathing. No one will even know you're using this tool! That's part of the beauty of it.

To practice, begin by thinking of a favorite, calm memory or of a peaceful place, like floating on an inflatable raft in a warm pool or lying on the beach on a sunny day. Use all your senses. What do you see? Look for the colors, shapes, people, or animals near you and far away. What do you hear? Are there birds chirping or waves crashing? Are there any smells, like the ocean or fresh cut grass? Can you taste anything? Walk closer to the sea and taste some of the saltwater or take a sip of that ice-cold lemonade you're holding.

Lastly, how do things feel? Feel the coolness of the glass of ice-cold lemonade. Touch a soft flower petal or a hard rock and notice the texture. As you're imagining this wonderful and safe place, you might notice that upsetting or angry thoughts or images force their way into your beautiful scene. Don't try to ignore these thoughts, as they will only get louder or more intrusive the harder you try not to think them. Just let them in and refocus your attention on the beautiful calm scene you've created in your mind; or, place the thought on a cloud and watch it drift away.

> I like to use my imagination to calm my angry mind. My favorite way is to imagine folding the thought into a paper airplane, throwing it into the air, and watching it fly away from my calm scene. Once, I imagined the angry thought was a green drop of food coloring in a glass of water. I watched the green color spread in the water until the thought was weak and diluted.
>
> —Emma

Continue to sit with this image for a few minutes and notice how peaceful it feels. Enjoy a sense of calm and the absence of anger, irritation, and tension.

Count to Ten

Someone has probably told you to "count to ten" when you start to feel angry. Perhaps you've even tried it. This is a great tool, particularly if you combine it with slow deep breathing. Once you've practiced slow deep breathing for a while, just count each COOL-CALM cycle from one to ten by adding a number after each exhale: In (COOL), out (CALM): one. In (COOL), out (CALM): two. And so on. If you want, count back down again after you reach ten.

STOP

Unfortunately, anger doesn't stop to think before it shoots from zero to 60. It just accelerates and leaves you to deal with the consequences. That's because anger clouds your thinking and then you end up doing something that you wouldn't do if you were cool and calm. Sometimes waiting just 3 or 4 seconds is enough time to prevent you from doing something that you later regret. One of the easiest ways to slow anger is to STOP and give yourself time to think and perhaps use some of the tools you'll learn later in the book.

The best way to use STOP is as an automatic relaxation cue that signals your body to relax quickly and automatically while you wait for anger to pass. Two of the last three skills you have learned will help you practice STOP: slow deep breathing and counting to ten. Once you learn to STOP, you'll be able to calm your body and mind anywhere and at any time in a matter of seconds.

To learn to STOP, close your eyes and imagine a STOP sign in your mind's eye. Later, you may want to practice with your eyes open until you're confident that you can shift immediately into STOP when you're in a stressful or frustrating situation, such as a difficult conversation with a friend. With time and practice, just imaging the STOP sign can be enough to bring on relaxation that cools the anger in your body.

STOP IN YOUR MIND'S EYE

STEP 1: Close your eyes and in your mind, imagine the STOP sign. Think "one" or say it softly aloud while you take two to three deep, slow breaths. As you breathe, scan your body for tension and release the tension as you slowly exhale.

STEP 2: Continue to imagine the STOP sign, and think "two" or say it softly aloud while you take two to three deep, slow breaths. As you breathe, scan your body for tension and release the tension as you slowly exhale.

STEP 3: Continue to imagine the STOP sign, and think "three" or say it softly aloud while you take two to three deep, slow breaths. As you breathe, scan your body for tension and release the tension as you slowly exhale.

STEP 4: Continue this process as you count to ten.

The final step—or more advanced step—is to practice STOP in real-life situations that tend to bring on frustration and anger. For example, try doing it before you walk into math class (if math stresses you out or if you don't like your math teacher), or when have to deal with someone you don't like. With practice, you can calm your body before you enter real life situations that frustrate you just by imagining the word STOP in your mind's eye (or saying STOP quietly out loud). You can practice by first imagining a stressful situation, and then following the STOP steps from above.

Here are some common situations that tend to trigger frustration or anger for many teens:

- Before tests, performances, or athletic events.
- When hanging out with friends.
- When a teacher asks to speak with you.

- When friends don't respond to your texts immediately (or at all).
- When you have to hang out with someone you don't like or respect.

Daily practice is the best way to learn a new skill quickly, so decide on a time when you're free from distraction to practice your Calm Body Tools. This might be right before you leave for school or the last thing before bed at night. There is no right time, just the time that is right for you. Learning to calm your body and to do this quickly will take some practice. Use the Calm Body Practice Log on the next page to record your progress.

Put It All Together

Slow deep breathing, progressive muscle relaxation, positive imagery, counting to ten, and telling yourself to STOP are important tools to help you cool your tense and angry body. You may want to write down the steps for each of the relaxation tools and save them on a note in your phone or on an index card in your backpack or purse. That way, you can practice it anytime and anywhere. For some, it helps to practice these tools with another person such as a friend, parent, or therapist. Regardless of whether you chose to practice alone or with another person, begin by practicing for 10-15 minutes once or twice daily for two to four weeks until using these tools is easy and automatic.

CALM BODY PRACTICE LOG

Instructions: Practice the Calm Body tools (slow deep breathing, progressive muscle relaxation, finding a calm inner place, and count to ten) at least once each day. Some days you may want to practice just the slow deep breathing and count to ten tools, and other days you may want to practice just the progressive muscle relaxation and finding a calm inner place. However, the most important thing is to practice regularly. Each day you practice the calm body tools, write the tool you practiced and your tension level before you practice and immediately after you practice on a 0 to 10 scale (where 0 = not at all tense; 10 = extremely tense).

Day of Week	Calm Body Tools	Tension Level (Before)	Tension Level (After)
Monday			
Tuesday			
Wednesday			
Thursday			
Friday			
Saturday			
Sunday			

IN A NUTSHELL

When you're tense, stressed, or on edge, anger comes on fast and hard. Learning to calm your body is an important step in keeping your cool.

1. Slow deep breathing can be practiced daily to help you calm your body. Additionally, progressive muscle relaxation is a daily antidote to the tension that primes anger. Create a personalized progressive muscle relaxation routine and practice it every night.

2. Imagining a calm place is a fun and easy way to cool an angry body or to give yourself a little relaxation break.

3. Count to 10 while you breathe slowly and deeply. It can give you time to think before you act and it's an easy skill to learn and use. Don't forget to STOP.

CHAPTER 4

Cool Your Angry Thoughts

Take a moment to recall an event that really steamed you, something that really got your anger going. Talk to yourself the way you talked to yourself then: "He did it on purpose," "This is so unfair," "She thinks she's better than me." Are you feeling angry yet, even a little? Just hanging out with those thoughts can make you feel angry all over again. Angry thoughts fuel angry feelings. Now, imagine the event again and throw in a few cooling thoughts, such as: "He misunderstood me," or "Chill a little," or "I'm okay the way I am." What did you notice? Did you feel a little cooler? That's the power of thoughts. Some thoughts rev anger, and other thoughts slow it down. Learning to cool your angry thoughts is an important tool to handle zero-to-60 anger.

In this chapter, you'll learn the role of thoughts in fueling and cooling your anger.

Then you'll learn typical thinking traps that contribute to excessive anger and learn several tools you can use to change your angry thoughts to cool down.

Angry Thoughts

What you think or how you interpret a situation determines how you feel and act. Your mind has the capacity to generate many types of thoughts: helpful, neutral, or unhelpful. As you learned in Chapter 1, even angry thoughts can be helpful at times. For example, if a kid cuts in front of you while you're in line to see a movie, anger alerts you that something's wrong. You might feel a little angry but instantly think, "He probably didn't see the end of the line. He just made a mistake." This means your anger is likely low and reasonable. You can then calmly point out to the kid that the end of the line is behind you. In this case, angry thoughts are *helpful*. It alerts you that someone ignored your right and a little bit of anger helps you assert yourself to correct the wrong.

If you think, "This guy's a jerk. He cut in front of me on purpose," your anger is likely high and unreasonable. You might yell and push him out of line. That's when the trouble starts for you. This example of an angry thought is *unhelpful*. It fuels a lot of anger that causes you to act before you think. People with zero-to-60 anger have too many of these unhelpful angry thoughts, and these thoughts get them in trouble over and over again. Although you have other types of thoughts stored in your mind, it may seem like the angry thoughts are always playing at high volume. Try the experiment on page 56. It'll show you how your thoughts can heat or cool your anger.

Once you've finished the experiment, look at the table of angry thoughts and cool thoughts. Which do you think are angry and which are cool?

Identify Your Anger Thinking Traps

Zero-to-60 anger hits you when your thinking falls into unhelpful patterns. These unhelpful patterns are like traps that grab you and hold you. You might fall into many different anger thinking traps or only a few, but if you have zero-to-60 anger, you probably fall into them a lot. Some thinking traps are about assuming the worst of other people. Other traps are about expecting that people will always treat you fairly. As you get to know your typical thinking traps, you'll realize some of the traps overlap or sound similar. That's okay. It's not important whether you have just a few or many thinking traps, or how much they overlap. The most important thing is to become familiar with the ones that tend to fuel your zero-to-60 anger. You'll likely focus the thinking tools you'll learn on those. Although several traps in the list that follows include suggestions to help you step out of these thinking traps, you'll also learn specific tools to help you change any angry thought. Here's a list of common thinking traps for people with zero-to-60 anger:

- Jumping to conclusions.
- Binocular vision.
- Fallacy of fairness.
- The line.
- Shoulds, Need-Tos, and Have-Tos.
- Black-or-White.
- Fortune telling.
- Mind reading.
- Overgeneralization.
- End of the world.
- Justification.
- Need to be right.

A THOUGHT EXPERIMENT

Instructions: Think back to a recent situation that caused you to feel angry. Close your eyes and imagine it all over again. Where were you? Who was there? What was going on? What were you feeling in your body? What angry self-talk was going through your mind? Rate the level of anger you're feeling from 0 to 10, where 10 is boiling hot.

Look at the example before you try this yourself.

Here's an example:

Step 1   Describe the situation: *My dad made me clean my room before I could shoot hoops with my friends.*

Step 2   Identify your angry self-talk and repeat that to yourself over and over again: *I hate him! He is such a control freak. He doesn't care about me. I'm just his slave.*

Step 3   Rate the level of anger (0 to 10): 5

Step 4   Now, talk to yourself but this time use some cool self-talk over and over again: *Cool down a little. It'll be okay. It won't take long. Keep your cool and you'll get to hang out with your friends soon.*

Step 5   Re-rate the level of anger (0 to 10): 3

Now you try it:

Step 1   Describe the situation:

Step 2   Identify your angry self-talk and repeat that to yourself over and over again:

Step 3   Rate the level of anger (0 to 10):

Step 4   Now, talk to yourself but this time use some cool self-talk over and over again:

Step 5   Re-rate the level of anger (0 to 10):

Jumping to Conclusions

When you were a kid, did you ever go outside with friends, lay on the ground, and look at clouds? It's a monkey. No, it's a unicorn. No, it's a monkey riding a unicorn. You and your friends looked at the same cloud but saw different things. The same is true for life: People often see the same situation differently. Different people have different views of a problem, in part, because they have

> I've always had some angry thoughts playing in my mind, but they really got worse when I started at the new school. It's hard for me to get to know new people. Every time a girl looked at me, I assumed she was judging me, which pissed me off. I walked around every day fuming and even when some of the girls said hello, I ignored them. One day, a girl asked me if I was okay. She thought I didn't like her. That blew me away. I was sure that the other girls hated ME. So I tried to change my thinking. I kept reminding myself that the other girls probably weren't judging me, that they had been worried about the same things—ME judging THEM! Even just thinking this made me start to feel a little better. I wasn't so angry at the others, which made me a little less nervous around them. One day, I smiled at a couple of the girls in my math class, and later they asked if they could sit next to me at lunch.
> —Camila

different goals or motives. When we get into arguments with people, it's often because we don't know what they really want or think. We have the wrong idea about where they're coming from. Our minds jump to conclusions and if you have zero-to-60 anger, your mind jumps to the conclusion that whatever the person

ANGRY THOUGHTS AND COOL THOUGHTS

did that made you mad, they did on purpose. In an instant and without thinking, your mind assumes their motive was to hurt or upset you. Most of the time there's another reason for a person's actions.

> **❝** I really like previews in the movie theatre. I always try to get there early so I can catch them. But Calvin thinks they're a waste of time—he just wants to see the movie he came for. So he likes to arrive just as the previews are ending. The last time we went to a movie together, I got there early (of course) and bought the tickets, and I was waiting and waiting for him, and getting angrier and angrier because I knew I was missing the previews. My anger thoughts started playing: "This is just like him. He's doing this on purpose to make me miss the previews." But when I went back and thought about motives, of course I realized that his motive wasn't to hurt me—he just didn't prioritize previews like I did. His goal was just to get there before the movie started. We both should've planned better ahead of time.
> —Jamal

It's okay to have motives and goals, and it's okay that you want to get what you want, but there are other goals you might want to consider. For example, staying out of trouble, keeping friends who like you, getting along with your mom and dad, your teachers, and perhaps even with your siblings. When your mind tends to jump to the conclusion that a person's motive or goal is to hurt you, then you're angry. And if you yell, scream, or hit someone because you're angry, then before you know it you're grounded, or you've lost another friend. That's why it's important to understand a person's intentions before you act in response to what the person did or said. Did he do it on purpose, or was it an accident? Did she do it because she hates you or because she didn't consider the effect her actions would have on you? Most arguments with other people—friends, teachers, parents, and siblings—are often because you didn't really know what the person wanted or was thinking. When you fall into the *Jumping to Conclusions* thinking trap, try gathering facts and building a conclusion rather than jumping to a conclusion. Granted, sometimes people say or do things on purpose (or even on accident!) that still are not OK and it's smart to talk about these things. But once you've gathered all the facts and take your time to respond, you're more likely to have a calm and productive discussion about the actual issue rather than a knock-down-drag-out fight about what you *think* is the issue.

Binocular Vision

The *Binocular Vision* thinking trap includes two types of thinking. It's like when you look through binoculars. When you look through one end of the binoculars, everything is magnified. When you look through the other end, everything shrinks. *Magnifying* means your mind makes things bigger than they really are. Your mind blows things out of proportion. For example, if a friend stands you up, it feels like the most important thing that has ever happened to you and you fume night and day for weeks. If your significant other breaks up with you, you think you'll never recover from it.

Shrinking, on the other hand, means your mind makes everything look smaller. You ignore the positives of people and don't give them the benefit of the doubt. You think, "He's always mean to me," when he's not; or, "My parents never give me a break," when, on occasion, they do. *Shrinking* can cause you to put a person into a box with a label, "He's an idiot," or "She's a selfish know-it-all." Labels fuel anger and before you know it, you're calling people the names you've labeled them.

Some teens apply the *Shrinking* thinking trap to themselves. They might shrink their accomplishments and strengths. They might think, "I can't do anything right," when they do, or "I'm horrible to my friends," when they often do nice things for them. The *Shrinking* thinking trap takes a toll on self-esteem and self-confidence.

Fallacy of Fairness

The *Fallacy of Fairness* thinking trap comes up a lot in the minds of teens with zero-to-60 anger. For example, when your parents expect you home earlier than your older sister, you might think, "That's not fair," and then resent your parents and your sister. When your teacher gives you a lower grade than your friend, you might think that's unfair too. When you're angry because you think that you didn't get your fair share or get a fair shake, you may have fallen into the *Fallacy of Fairness* thinking trap. When it comes to fairness, what is or isn't fair is often in the eye of the beholder. For example, your parents likely think it's fair to expect you home a bit earlier than your older sister, although you don't. Your teacher likely thinks your grade is fair and appropriate for you and a higher grade was appropriate for your friend.

This is why fairness is a fallacy. Wanting others to treat you fairly is a good thing and you're entitled to want it, but *expecting others to always treat you fairly*, according to what *you* determine is fair or unfair, will only fuel you anger over and over again. If you tend to fall into this thinking trap, remind yourself that life isn't always fair, or at least not fair the way you see it, and, that resenting the unfairness of life only adds to your stress and anger. And then move on.

The Line

The Line thinking trap is when you draw a line in the sand. You set an arbitrary limit or standard and expect people to follow it at all times, whether they think it's reasonable or not. When people cross the line, it's unacceptable and then you're angry. For example, following a breakup with your boyfriend, you might expect a friend to ask you how you're feeling every time she sees you. When she doesn't, you think, "That's it. I told her I'm having a hard time and she ignores me." Although it's your right to wish to be treated a certain way, expecting people to follow this standard at all times and in all circumstances sets you up to feel a lot of unnecessary frustration and resentment. If you tend to fall into *The Line* thinking trap, try to be more flexible. People aren't perfect and no matter how hard they try to do the right thing, they'll sometimes fail. Accepting their imperfections can help you feel less angry and resentful.

Shoulds, Need-Tos, and Have-Tos

The *Shoulds*, *Need-Tos*, and *Have-Tos* thinking trap can snag you when other people don't meet your expectations. *Shoulds* are the rules you have for a situation. When you fall into this thinking trap, you might think people should be nice to you or they should do things the way you do them. You might think your best friend should have to study like you rather than have fun with friends. You might have rules about what's right or wrong and people— friends, teachers, parents—keep breaking them. They probably don't even know about your rules. And, don't forget the *shoulds* in sheep's clothing. These are the *need-tos* and *have-tos*. These are expectations too. *He needs to stop talking in class. You have to call me tonight.* Every time someone breaks one of your rules, your anger increases until it shoots from zero to 60 in an instant.

At times, you might even apply these rules to yourself. You might think of all the things you should have done or have to do. You might think, "I have to always get good grades," or, "Everyone should like me all the time." The *shoulds* or *have-tos* are too much. You've set the bar too high for yourself—for anyone, really—so you begin to worry whether you'll be able to do it. You work constantly to meet these expectations, but because you expect too much of yourself, you fail. Pretty soon, you're less confident. You start to wonder if you can do things—even easy things you've done before. Your life becomes stressful and not a lot of fun. You begin to feel irritated with little things. You start to feel down because it's all work and no play. You start to resent your friends who have time for fun and you snap at them. The *Shoulds, Need-Tos* and *Have-Tos* thinking trap weakens your self-confidence and self-esteem, and fuels your anger.

Black-or-White

The *Black-or-White* thinking trap is either all this way or all that way. This thinking trap ignores everything in between. It's black-or-white thinking and it fuels anger. You might think, "He's either my friend or he's my enemy." However, this person— like lots of people you know—is likely somewhere in between. Sometimes he's neither your friend nor your enemy. He's just who he is. The truth is that most situations are somewhere in the middle—neither horrible nor perfect. Friends are neither good nor bad. Teachers are neither brilliant nor idiots.

When you fall into this thinking trap, it's impossible for you to see the full picture of people or situations. Your mind filters out the positives and over-focuses on the negatives of a person. Your mind dwells on what the person did to upset you, and it's difficult for you to see the good things the person has done for you. This fuels bitterness and resentment. The people in your life become caricatures of who they really are as your mind thinks, "She only cares about herself," "He's insensitive," or "There he goes again, always late."

Fortune Telling

When you fall into the *Fortune Telling* thinking trap, you believe that you can predict the future. Although you might be able to predict some things, such as, "My mom won't serve ice cream for dinner tonight," most of the time you can't predict things very well. When you fall into the *Fortune Telling* thinking trap, you typically predict friends will mistreat you before they do, or your parents will ground you before they've even spoken to you. Once you're in this trap, you feel resentful and angry before anyone has done or said anything. Is it any wonder you snap at a friend when you've predicted he's going to be mean? Instead, remind yourself that even if some of your past predictions were true, it happened by chance rather than because you actually have a sixth sense.

Mind Reading

Some people believe they can read minds. Well, not really, but they do believe they know the intentions of people or what people are thinking. *Mind Reading* is a common thinking trap, but once again, just because you believe you can read minds doesn't mean you can. No one can read other people's minds. If you find yourself *guessing* what others think, then you've fallen into the *Mind Reading* thinking trap. For example, you're convinced you know what your boyfriend is thinking and planning to do: "He's going to break up with me." You feel hurt and angry. You decide to show him you don't care. You yell at him and break off the relationship before he does.

Overgeneralization

When you take one small thing and use it to draw conclusions about lots of other things, you've fallen into the *Overgeneralization* thinking trap. This is similar to the *Jumping to Conclusions* trap. It's like thinking that you've ruined the cookie batter when you added one teaspoon more of sugar than what the recipe called for, or that if you miss a single pass in football game the coach will cut you from the team. When your mind falls into the *Overgeneralization* thinking trap, you feel resentful and angry about the smallest thing. But many factors contribute to what happens in life, not just one thing and, particularly, not just one small thing.

End of the World

The *End of the World* thinking trap convinces you that the most recent hurt or disappointment is horrible or it's the most important event in your life. The *End of the World* thinking trap intensifies your anger and creates a lot of stress and worry too because you're always watching for the next big hurt or disappointment. For example, your friend has let you down several times before, and it always hurts, but this time you believe it's horrible, unbearable, and the most important event in your life. Your anger builds as you "horribilize" the hurt. It's too much. You'll never recover from this one. It's the end of your world as you know it.

Justification

The *Justification* thinking trap assumes that you always have a good reason for why you did what you did. You yelled at your friend because you're having a bad day. You pushed a girl because she's bossy. You have a reason or rationalization for every angry action, word, and deed. Many times you're correct. You were having a bad day. The girl is bossy. But even when you're right, deep down you can't justify zero-to-60 anger. Your reaction was out of proportion to the wrong done.

Need to Be Right

When you fall into the *Need to Be Right* thinking trap you're almost always headed into an argument, conflict, and anger. When you think this way, it's impossible to take no for an answer. You debate and insist your opinions are correct and your view is the only way to see things. You'll go to any length to be right and people know it. You can't tolerate the thought that you might be wrong or mistaken, because being wrong hits your self-esteem hard. But everyone is mistaken or wrong from time to time. Only people who are perfect are never wrong—and no one is perfect. Remember, being wrong doesn't make you stupid. It just means you're human, like the rest of the population. You can handle being wrong, and needing to be right gets in the way of making and keeping friends.

Did any of these thinking traps seem familiar as you read along? Perhaps all of them or perhaps just a few. Sometimes a single thought can have two thinking traps, such as, "I can't stand it. He'll never change." This is an example of *End of the World* and *Fortune Telling*.

For many people, anger thoughts play in the background and they're often not even aware they're there. Knowing that the thought, "She did it on purpose," is the *Jumping to Conclusions* thinking trap, for example, can nudge you to use some of the thinking tools you're about to learn.

To figure out your typical anger thinking traps, look at the ABCs of Anger forms you completed earlier. Read what you wrote in the Angry Thoughts column. Do these thoughts fit into a particular trap or traps? If yes, note the specific trap it matches. How often do you fall into one or more of these thinking traps?

Change Hot Thoughts to Cool Thoughts

Anger thoughts are hot thoughts. They make you boil. Now that you know how to catch them using the ABCs of Anger form and have identified the anger thinking traps you tend to fall into, it's time to learn tools to change these hot thoughts to cool thoughts. For example, when Alejandro's teacher gave him an F on a paper rather than letting him turn it in late, this hot thought raced through his mind: "That's totally unfair. He hates me and I hate him." This is the *Fallacy of Fairness* thinking trap that assumes others will and should always treat you "fairly." Alejandro caught this hot thought and decided to try coming up with cool thoughts to cool down: "I missed the deadline. Mr. Harvey warned me a couple of times—it's probably fair that he gave me an F. He wants me to learn from this. He's usually an okay guy. Maybe I'll ask him if there's something I could do to bring up my grade."

Learning to change your hot thoughts into cool thoughts takes some practice, but once you learn to do this, you'll see that this helps to cool your anger. You might want to use the calm body tools you've learned in this book first, such as doing deep breathing, or positive imagery, before you try to change the hot thought. Once you cool your angry body, it'll be easier to use the thinking tools described next.

The best tools to cool your angry thoughts are:

- Find the facts.

- Start the time machine.
- Move to another seat.
- Share a slice of the responsibility pie.
- Think it through to the end.
- Write a cool letter to your hot-tempered self.

Find the Facts

By now, you're probably pretty good at catching your hot thoughts. You've written those thoughts in the Angry Thoughts column on the ABCs of Anger forms you completed. As you look back over the forms, you'll likely see a few anger thinking traps. Although these hot thoughts might feel like facts, they're probably opinions. Facts are pieces of evidence about an event. Facts

> I never really questioned what I was thinking; I always just assumed it was true. I definitely never asked myself, "Where's the evidence?" Learning to find the facts helped me cool down a lot. I noticed that I usually jumped to conclusions that almost never had any facts to support them. Once I slowed down and looked for evidence that maybe my anger thought wasn't true, I started to feel more in control. I also started to notice that other kids sometimes don't know the difference between facts and opinions either. They acted as if what they thought was true—just like I did. Realizing that was a little thing, but it helped a lot.
> —Camila

are either correct or incorrect. Opinions, on the other hand, are the way we see things, which may or may not be true. Sometimes our facts about an event are correct, but our opinions about the facts are incorrect or blown out of proportion. For example, some students won't do as well as others on a test. That's just a fact. Thinking you're stupid because you didn't do as well on the test as others is an opinion. Finding the true facts of a situation can cool the hot thoughts that fuel your anger.

Find the Facts is a great tool because it helps you to focus on a more accurate and helpful view of the situation. Once you have all the facts, the hot thought can lose some of its power and your anger cools. Here's how to do it:

STEP 1: Get a piece of paper. Think back to your most recent anger outburst. Where were you? What were you doing? Who was there? Now, at the top of the page, write down your anger hot thought.

STEP 2: Rate how strongly you believe the anger thought is true, from 0 to 100 (where 100 means you believe it completely). Then, rate how angry you feel about the situation, from 0 to 10 (where 10 is enraged).

STEP 3: Use a T-chart to draw two columns in the middle of the page.

STEP 4: At the top of the left column, write True. In that column, list all the evidence you can think of that makes the anger thought true or correct.

STEP 5: At the top of the right column, write False. In that column, list all the evidence you can think of that makes the anger thought false or incorrect.

STEP 6: Now, look at the evidence listed in both columns. What do you think? Which pieces of evidence are more realistic? Does your original anger thought contain facts or opinions? If it seems to be an opinion, think of a thought that's more accurate about the situation.

STEP 7: At the bottom of your T-chart, write down your new cool thought.

STEP 8: Re-rate how strongly you believe the anger thought and how much anger you feel now.

Evaluating the evidence for and against an anger thought is exactly how a jury uses information presented by defendant's attorney and the plaintiff's attorney to arrive at a verdict. Be sure you don't confuse a feeling, which is similar to an opinion, with a fact. This is like the defense attorney saying to the judge, "Your honor. My client isn't guilty of robbery because I feel like he would never do something like that."

> Well, my dad does insist I finish my homework before I can go out. That's a fact. But when I start thinking he's doing it just to make my life miserable...I can't read his mind, so I guess that's just an opinion. And thinking that definitely makes me more likely to get angry.
> —Emma

If you're having trouble finding evidence the anger thought is false, ask yourself three questions: *What makes me think this*

JASON'S FIND THE FACTS EXERCISE

Angry thought	Belief Level	Anger Level
My dad just wants to make my life miserable. He'll never change.	85	8

True	False
He makes me do my homework before I hang out with friends.	Last Saturday, he drove me and my friends to a movie. He comes to all my games and takes me and friends out for pizza after practices. He's backed off about homework on weekends. He knows school is tough for me. He used to be really impatient with me but now that he understands that I'm really trying, he's a lot more patient.

New thought	Belief Level	Anger Level
Sometimes my dad and I disagree about what's best for me, but he doesn't want me to be miserable. He knows school's not my thing and that's why he encourages me to play sports and learn computer programming. He just wants me to be successful so that I can get a good job when I grow up.	65	3

Thinking Trap

Jumping to Conclusions

Fortune Telling

thought is true? Is there any evidence that this thought might not be true, or not completely true? Is there another way of looking at this situation? Also, ask yourself what you would tell a friend if the friend was in this situation. Sometimes it's easier to see things clearly and objectively when we evaluate someone else's situation. If you're still having trouble finding evidence, ask a parent or friend to help you evaluate both sides—true and false—of the anger thought. The *Find the Facts* tool works great for most anger thoughts, so give it a try. With practice, this tool will become second nature to you.

Start the Time Machine

Time is a great salve for angry feelings. A lot of times, whatever made you angry seems less important after some time has passed. For example, when your best friend spills milk on your new sweater, you'll probably feel intensely angry because this event feels intensely important when it happens. But after a week, a little milk on your sweater will seem less important and your anger will cool. The *Time Machine* is a great way to change your thinking when you've made a mountain out of a molehill. Time provides perspective. The *Time Machine* works well for other feelings too, such as hurt, guilt, anxiety, or embarrassment.

Move to Another Seat

Imagine you're seated in a large theater. You look around and notice that, depending on where you sit, you have different views or perspectives of the stage. There's the mezzanine, the orchestra, the balcony. Every perspective is a bit different and, for that reason, you have a different experience of the performance. This works for thoughts too. When you don't have all the facts, your mind is more likely to jump to the familiar conclusion that people did what they did on purpose. Just because your mind jumps

START THE TIME MACHINE

Event: What happened to make you angry?

1 Couldn't care less	Rate anger level (0 to 10, where 10 is boiling) *before* you start the Time Machine:
2 Definitely not important	Now, ask yourself the following questions and rate with the importance scale on the left.
3 Mildly important	How important is this event in the moment?
4 Almost important	How important will this event be in an hour?
5 Important, but not life changing	How important will this event be in a day?
6 Important, but I have bigger fish to fry	How important will this event be in a week?
7 Important, and I will take it seriously	How important will this event be in a month?
	How important will this event be in a year?
8 Very important	How important will this event be in 5 years?
9 Very, very important	How important will this event be in 10 years?
10 My life depends on this	Re-rate anger level (0 to 10, where 10 is boiling) *after* you stop the Time Machine:

to this conclusion quickly and automatically doesn't mean you can't learn to slow it down and view the situation from other perspectives. It just takes some practice.

> " When I heard that Jacelle invited Betsy to hang out and didn't ask me, I went ballistic. Jacelle's my best friend and I couldn't understand why she would do that.
> I was fuming all night long. Then I remembered the Time Machine. At first, this felt like the most important thing in my life but then, as I started the Time Machine, it felt a little less important, and my anger started to cool. By the time I asked myself how important this would be in a month or a year, I realized I probably wouldn't even remember it. I still want to talk to Jacelle, but now that I feel cooler, I think I'll be able to ask her about it rather than blow up at her. There's probably a good reason. I tried the Time Machine with embarrassment too and it worked great. The other day, I tripped in front of a guy I like. I felt really embarrassed, an end-of-the-world kind of embarrassment. I started the Time Machine for that too and it helped. I didn't think about it all night and I was able to talk to him the next day.
> —Ayanna "

HIDDEN MOTIVES

Situation: I'm taking a math test and my pencil is on my desk next to my test booklet. The kid next to me hits my desk with his hand, which makes the pencil roll off my desk and on to the floor.

The "to be mean" motive: He knocked my pencil onto the floor to bug me.

Other Motives

To Help

The pencil was already rolling but I hadn't noticed; the kid tried to catch the pencil but missed.

An Accident

The other kid was just stretching, and accidentally knocked the desk.

Situation: I'm carrying my lunch on a tray as I walk toward my friends to sit with them. There is a big puddle of chocolate milk on the floor in front of me. As I walk by another group of kids, a girl jumps up and bumps my tray. My plate of spaghetti and meatballs falls onto my new white shoes.

The "to be mean" motive: She did that on purpose. She hates that I have new shoes and wants to ruin them.

Other Motives

To Help

The girl jumped up quickly to try and wipe the milk off the floor so that I didn't slip.

An Accident

The girl just didn't see me and bumped into my tray accidentally.

It's not always clear which reason is the real reason. That's because you don't know the person's goal or motive. The motive of the person in each of these situations isn't clear, is it?

This is where the *Move to Another Seat* tool can help. Imagine that theater again. You decide to move from section to section in the theater. Each time you look at the stage, you have a slightly different experience.

To practice using the *Move to Another Seat* tool, you can practice stepping back and thinking through the goals or motives of people. We get into arguments when we assume we know the motives of people when we don't. People with zero-to-60 anger tend to assume they know where other people are coming from. They also assume the person intended to hurt them or do something bad to them on purpose. Most of the time there's another reason or reasons for why people did what they did, and it's usually because they have a goal or motive you don't know. Typically, people do what they do for three reasons:

- To be mean.
- To help.
- Accidentally (therefore it wasn't a goal or a motive).

Let's practice Moving to Another Seat with Ayanna and Alejandro.

> I was just about to leave for school in my new outfit when mom told me to go change. Change! This outfit is amazing. She doesn't know what she's talking about. I left anyway, but then my first-period teacher told me I was breaking the dress code and had to change. I told him what I thought of the so-called "dress code." Who are they to tell me what I can and can't wear? That should be my choice! Well. He sent me to the principal, and it just kept escalating from there.
> —Ayanna

Ayanna's goal or motive was to express herself. Who can argue with that? Her mom, her teacher, and the principal had other goals that competed with Ayanna's goal to express herself. Although Ayanna's goal is important—who doesn't want to express what they like and admire about themselves?—Ayanna has other goals, too. Ayanna wants to do well in school, but refusing to attend classes will make it hard for her to do that. She wants to hang out with friends, but she can't if her mother grounds her. She doesn't want to upset the principal because she wants him to write a letter of recommendation to help her get into college.

The principal wants Ayanna, as well as all the other students, to follow all the school rules, including the dress code, because if he didn't enforce the school rules then parents, teachers, and other students might complain to the school board. He might then lose his job.

The teacher wants Ayanna to follow school rules, because if he doesn't enforce the dress code, he might lose his job.

Ayanna's mom wants her to do well in school and she's worried that the school will expel her. She knows about the dress code and is worried that the school will send Ayanna home and then Ayanna will fall behind with her schoolwork.

> **"** I was trying to finish my math homework before it got dark, so I would have time to go kick a ball around with my friends. But then my dad comes in and harps on me about how I'm not doing well in math, and I should do EXTRA problems to practice!

I'm already working so hard, but apparently it's not good enough for him! We started arguing, and then my sister came in and told me to be quiet because she was trying to study and our mom had a migraine. So it's all my fault now, I guess.
—Alejandro

99

In the next situation, Alejandro's goal is to play soccer with his friends. Alejandro knows he's not a strong student, but he's okay with that. He's the best athlete in the school and he wants to play college soccer and—who knows—maybe make it into the pros. But Alejandro has other goals, too. He wants to do well enough in school to get into college, and getting better grades in math will help with that. He wants to spend as much time playing soccer as possible, but he can't do that if his dad grounds him for the weekend. He wants to continue playing on the high school soccer team, but he has to keep up his grades to do that.

Alejandro's dad wants him to try hard to do well in school. He wants Alejandro to have good enough grades to go to college whether he gets an athletic scholarship or not.

Alejandro's mom wants it to be quiet in the house when she has a migraine. Noise makes it hard for her to recover and to work the next day. She's worried that she's missing too much time from work and that the company might fire her.

Alejandro's sister is falling behind in her studies. She has learning difficulties and it's all she can do to focus. The noise doesn't help. She just wants a quiet environment so that she can concentrate.

Although Ayanna and Alejandro have great goals, it'll be hard for them to reach those goals if they don't learn to cool their anger. Sometimes it helps to try and see behind other people's actions, and think about what motives might be hidden.

> " I probably use the Move to Another Seat tool more than any other. I realized that I almost always assume that my friends, parents, and teachers have it out for me. I jump to the 'she did it on purpose' conclusion even though I don't have any facts to back it up. I now realize that people have different motives for what they do, and that's okay. I have motives too. Sure, some people do things on purpose and sometimes to be mean, but that doesn't happen much. I need to give people the benefit of the doubt. I've been trying hard to assume that people's motives are good and that they don't intentionally do things to hurt or upset me—especially my friends and family.
> —Jason "

Share a Slice of the Responsibility Pie

Almost nothing is just one person's fault. Life is more complicated than that. Sometimes it's easier to blame someone for what happened than it is to take responsibility for your part in it. Yes, it may be a very small part, but it's still your part. Blaming other people doesn't resolve conflict. It just makes it worse. The *Share a Slice of the Responsibility Pie* is a great tool when you tend to blame other people for things that happen in life. Stepping back and looking at the big picture redistributes responsibility and, therefore, redistributes the blame. Taking your share, and only your share, and giving the other person his or her share can quickly cool your anger. Follow these steps to *Share a Slice of the Responsibility Pie*:

STEP 1: Think of a recent upsetting situation when you blamed someone for what happened. For example, "It's all his fault that we're late," or, "It's all her fault that my phone is broken."

STEP 2: List as many factors as possible that contributed to the upsetting outcome. Begin the list with yourself and end the list with the person who you think deserves all the responsibility and blame.

STEP 3: Go to the top of the list and assign yourself a percentage that represents your estimate of how much you contributed (or will contribute) to the event. This is your slice of the responsibility pie.

STEP 4: Go down the list and assign a percentage of the pie to all the other factors. Make certain the total percentage adds up to 100%.

STEP 5: Review all the factors and their percentage of responsibility. Compare this to your percentage and to the percentage for the person you thought was at fault. What percent responsible are you compared to all the other factors?

STEP 6: Using this new information, write out a more accurate cool thought that accounts for all the factors and not just a particular person or thing.

> I was fuming because Julie made us late to the movie, but when I looked at all the responsibilities, I had to admit it wasn't all her fault that we missed the beginning. Julie actually tried really hard to get to the movie on time. There were a lot of things that she couldn't control. They just happened. That's usually the case, isn't it? I felt less angry at Julie after I realized that. I've used this tool when I'm hard on myself sometimes, too. Rather than blaming myself when something doesn't work out, I step back and look at the slices of the responsibility pie. It actually makes me feel better.
>
> —Emma

EMMA'S SHARE A SLICE OF THE RESPONSIBILITY PIE EXERCISE

Angry Thought: It's all Julie's fault that we missed the first part of the movie.
Anger Level Before (0 to 10): 7

Situation: I was standing in front of the movie theater waiting for Julie. She was late and I kept texting her but she didn't get back to me. The signal was weak so I walked up the block to get a stronger signal. Finally, Julie arrived but I didn't see her until I walked back to the theater. By that time we had missed the first 20 minutes of the movie. Julie apologized and told me that her 3-year old brother found her phone and put it someplace. She couldn't find it. Her mother helped look for it too but she couldn't find it either. When she found her phone the battery was low. She has an old phone and it's difficult to charge fully. Julie thought she would charge her phone with the charger they kept in the car. As she and her mom were driving to the movie, Julie couldn't find the charger. Her mom told her that she'd taken it out of the car to use at work and she forgot to put it back in the car.

Factor	Responsibility (%)
I walked a few blocks away from the theater and didn't see Julie arrive.	5%
Julie's brother lost her phone.	20%
Julie and her mom didn't search the house carefully enough.	20%
Julie's phone is old and doesn't take a good charge.	10%
Julie's mother took the charger out of the car and forgot to return it.	20%
My phone signal was weak.	15%
Traffic.	10%

New thought: Hey, stuff happens. It wasn't all Julie's fault. There's plenty of blame to go around: little brothers, moms, old phones, and weak cell signals.
Anger Level After (0 to 10): 2

Think It Through to the End

In order to win at certain games, it's necessary to think ahead. Thinking ahead and thinking through to the end is how you avoid losing when playing checkers, chess, or Jenga. In any of these games, if you don't plan ahead, you're going to lose. The Jenga tower crashes down; your checker gets jumped; your king gets taken. That's it, game over! There are consequences to losing control of your temper too. You can lose friends, lose fun, and sometimes lose bigger things in the future, such as college and a good job.

Thinking through each decision before acting is how you win at Jenga, chess, or checkers. It's also how you win at life. Anger can interfere with your ability to think ahead and consider all possible consequences for an action. If you're like most teens, you mostly worry about getting in trouble because of how you act. There are other consequences too, such as how your actions affect other people. Will other kids start to hate you because you hurt their feelings? Will your teachers stop caring whether you do well in school or not because they've given up on you? Learning to think ahead helps you treat people with care and respect. It takes practice to build this mental habit, particularly if you want to think ahead quickly and automatically. That's how the *Think It Through to the End* tool can help. With practice, you can learn to think ahead calmly and clearly before you act on a decision. The best way to do this is to remember several anger events from the recent past and train your mind to think through your actions to the end until this occurs quickly and automatically. Follow these steps to practice:

STEP 1: Look at several of the ABCs of Anger forms you completed. You can also think back to a recent event in which you felt very angry and recall who was there, what you were doing, and what the other people were doing.

STEP 2: Identify what you wanted at that moment.

STEP 3: Identify what the other person wanted at that moment.

STEP 4: Describe what happened. What did you do? What did the other person do? What happened then?

STEP 5: Now, describe the troubles or consequences you experienced after the angry actions. To help you remember consequences, check the list of Anger Minuses in Chapter 2.

STEP 6: Think through what you could have done differently in the situation. Identify any tools you could have used that would have helped.

To see how this is done, check out the Jamal's *Think It Through to the End* exercise.

JAMAL'S *THINK IT THROUGH* EXERCISE

What did you want?

It was my turn to play my video game. I wanted to play the game with Joe, my friend. My little brother was playing his video game and wouldn't give me the game controller.

What did you do?

I screamed at him and grabbed the controller. It broke into three pieces.

What did the other person want?

My brother wanted 10 minutes more to play his video game until the end of the scene.

What consequences did you experience?

Self-image: I felt like a total loser. I should be able to keep my cool and I lost it again!

Money: Dad made me pay for the controller.

Friends: Joe said he was embarrassed and didn't want to hang out with me at my house. Dad grounded me for the weekend and I couldn't hang out with friends.

Schoolwork: Dad made me do extra math homework all week.

Family: Dad gave me "the lecture." My brother said he's scared of me.

What could you have done differently?

I could have waited 10 minutes. If my brother didn't stop his game after 10 minutes I could ask my dad to tell my brother to give me the controller.

Write a Cool Letter to Your Hot-Tempered Self

Write a Cool Letter to Your Hot-Tempered Self is another tool that teaches you to stop and think through the consequences of a decision before you act. First, check the ABCs of Anger forms and identify one or two situations in which you acted before thinking. Next, now that you're cool and can think through the event calmly and clearly, write a letter to your hot-tempered self. In the letter, describe what happened, what you learned, and what you could do differently next time. The more cool letters that you write to your hot-tempered self, the more your mind will remember to think through a decision quickly and automatically before you act.

As you write, remember this: don't turn the anger against yourself. Write a letter that is caring and compassionate, that inspires you to work hard at managing the anger, that helps you act differently and want to act differently in the future. Write a letter that convinces yourself that you can do it.

Dear Hot-Tempered Emma,

Last Tuesday you yelled at Julie in history class because she took your phone while you were texting Martin. You grabbed at the phone to get it back and accidentally hit her in the chin with your hand. Julie screamed and started to cry. Mr. Jameson was angry and told Julie and you to go to the principal's office. It was a big scene and the principal sent you both home and told you that you couldn't attend the school dance on Saturday.

Julie's parents grounded her for the week. Your parents grounded you for two weeks. Now, Julie isn't speaking to you. When you say hello, she walks away. Your friends feel really awkward when they're around you and Julie, so they don't really want to hang out with you.

You feel terrible about what happened. Julie's your best friend and she took your phone because she thinks Martin's not good for you. Even though you don't agree with her about Martin, you can see now that she was just trying to be your friend and do the right thing.

Emma, the most important thing is to fix things with Julie. Go to her and apologize. Tell her that you're sorry that you yelled at her and you know she did it because she cares about you. In the future, Emma, think through the effects of anger on your friends and your friendships. You care about your friends and they care about you. You can handle the anger. Just keep working at it. If your friends know that you're working hard to learn to stay cool, then they'll hang in there with you. You can do this, Emma! I'm on your side.

Very sincerely,

Cool Emma

IN A NUTSHELL

Anger thoughts run hot through the minds of people with zero-to-60 anger. These anger thoughts play loud and long and tend to cloud your ability to think clearly and act calmly. That's how the cool thought tools in this chapter can help. After applying the tools for a few weeks, you might notice you catch hot thoughts faster and you're better at thinking through decisions before you act. This means the process of changing anger thoughts is becoming automatic and you're building and strengthening a new mental habit.

1. Remember to identify and record your particular anger thinking traps. Knowing your thinking traps can help you quickly catch the anger before it builds and you act before you think.

2. Don't forget to use the ABCs of Anger forms. Make copies of the forms or add Notes to your phone or laptop and keep them handy. When something makes you angry, complete an ABCs of Anger form. Then, as soon as you can, use one of the tools to change your anger thoughts to cool thoughts.

3. After you use the tools several times, decide which tools work the best for you.

CHAPTER 5

Stop the Drumbeat of Anger

You learned in Chapter 1 about angry actions. There are physical angry actions like yelling and hitting. These are aggressive behaviors. But there's another type of angry action no one can see and from which only you suffer. That's the drumbeat of anger, or anger rumination. Anger rumination is a mental action where you repeatedly and relentlessly think about and dwell on the situation that made you angry to begin with. For example, if a friend stands you up for a movie date, you think about it all night, over and over: "She only cares about herself." "She thinks she's too good for me." "She's a jerk." When you dwell on a situation all night long and it's the first thing you think about when you wake up in the morning, your anger just builds and builds. When you see your friend the next day at school, the anger shoots from zero to 60 in seconds and then you yell at her. Perhaps you call her a name. That's what happens when you beat the drum of anger all day and all night: more anger and more conflict.

To see how anger rumination increases your anger, try this. Close your eyes and think back to an old grudge. Perhaps a friend stood you up or your teacher accused you of something you didn't do. Let yourself imagine it all over again. On a 0 to 10 scale (where 10 is blowing up angry), rate how angry you feel. Not too angry, right? Now, imagine the hurt or embarrassment you felt. Allow your mind to go to the whys. Why did she say that? Why did he do that? Dwell on the unfairness of the situation. Tell yourself over and over that it wasn't fair or that it wasn't right. Now, re-rate your anger. Did it increase a little?

In this chapter, you'll learn ten tools to quiet the drumbeat of anger rumination:

- Distract Yourself.
- Watch the Drumbeat.
- Write It Down.
- Schedule Drum Practice.
- Laugh a Little.
- Walk a Minute in Their Shoes.
- Savor the Good and Pleasant.
- Find the Good Thing in Someone.
- Practice Caring and Compassion Toward Yourself.
- Forgive.

It's not easy to stop anger rumination. Our minds are wired to do this and after a while, rumination can become a habit—a mental habit—and like all habits, mental habits are difficult to break. However, with some practice, you can learn to break it. The key is to use the tools early, when you're just beginning to ruminate and before you lose your cool. The longer you wait to slow the drumbeat, the harder it is to stop it. It's all about getting ahead of anger rumination before it builds. Also, many of the tools in this chapter will help you slow the drumbeat of other feelings, such as anxiety or sadness. Rumination can intensify these feelings, too.

Distract Yourself

Perhaps the simplest tool to slow anger rumination is to distract yourself from the thoughts, memories, and images of the situation on which your mind wishes to dwell. Distraction is easy and perhaps the quickest way to take your mind away from the pull you feel to beat the drum. There are many ways to distract yourself, but one of the best ways is to engage in an activity, such as a hobby or sport. Experiment with types of distraction until you find some that work best for you.

WAYS TO DISTRACT YOURSELF FROM THE DRUM BEAT

Listen to fun music.	Call and chat with someone.	Hang out with a friend.	Take a hot shower.	Hold a piece of ice.	Name objects in the room (e.g., chair, table, light).
Watch a funny or up-lifting movie or TV show.	Slowly eat something that you like.	Watch funny videos.	Watch clouds or the leaves move in a tree.	Jog or walk your dog.	Dance in your room.
Write a story or poem.	Count your breaths or steps.	Count backward from 100.	Groom your pet.	Play a game on your phone.	Read one of your favorite books.
Draw or paint.	Walk around the neighbor-hood.	Splash cold water on your face or take a cold shower.	Do yoga.	Shoot some hoops or kick around a soccer ball.	Look at photos of fun times with friends.

Watch the Drumbeat

As you've learned, the more you think or hang out with anger thoughts, the more tense your body feels, and the more likely it is that your anger will intensify. Watching the drumbeat of anger is a way to distance yourself both from what you're thinking and what you're feeling in your body. Watching is not the same as relaxing, although you may feel relaxed as you practice. You don't have to do anything but watch your anger thoughts and feelings. As you watch the drumbeat, notice how angry thoughts and feelings come and go. Allow them to change without avoiding or judging them. Try not to criticize or blame yourself for the drumbeat. That's the way minds work. Just notice the thoughts and feelings and let them go. If you're distracted by something, notice it and gently bring your attention back to your breath as you learned earlier in Chapter 3.

WATCH THE DRUM BEAT

1. Get into a comfortable position. You can sit in a comfortable chair or lie on your bed. Close your eyes.

2. *Focus on the breath*: Breathe in and then breathe out. Notice but don't change the rise and fall of your belly. Observe the movement of your breath like a balloon inflating and deflating.

3. *Feet*: Bring awareness to your feet. Notice any sensations: coolness, dryness, tingling, warmth. Notice and accept whatever sensation you feel in that part of your body.

4. *Legs*: Move your attention from your feet up your legs. Notice any sensations in your ankles, calves, thighs, and then up to your hips. Bring your awareness to any sensation in your legs.

5. *Hips, abdomen, chest*: Move your attention to your hips and to the organs in your abdomen and chest. Notice the sensations in your joints. Feel your skin and muscles in this area.

6. *Lower, then upper back*: Move your attention to your back. Begin with the lowest vertebra and scan slowly, one by one, each vertebra of your spine. Notice your ribs expand with each breath. Notice your heartbeat.

7. *Shoulders*: Move your attention up to your shoulders. Gradually move your attention down each arm, then your wrists, and hands. Notice the tips of your fingers and your fingernails. Move your attention up your neck and to the back of your head.

8. *Face*: Move your attention to your face. Imagine a circle of awareness that moves up from your chin to your forehead. Become aware of the feelings in your chin, your jaw, your cheeks, and your eyes. Notice the sensations in and around your nose and mouth. Notice your ears and the feeling of hair on your head.

9. *Head*: Move from your forehead to the top of your head, then down to the back of your head and to your neck.

10. *Whole body*: Expand your awareness to your entire body. Open your awareness like the lens of a camera to take in your full body, from the tips of your toes to the tips of your fingers. Breathe in slowly and out slowly as you feel your entire body.

Write It Down

Writing rather than thinking is a great way to slow anger rumination. Sometimes rumination is your mind's way of figuring out how you feel. Unfortunately, trying to figure things out in your head just keeps the rumination going and your anger building. Writing helps you sort through the situation and your feelings about it. It can give you some distance from the event. An easy way to do this is to write a letter to an imaginary pen pal. So much about anger rumination is about someone else: what he said and what she did. Writing a letter to an imaginary pen pal helps you shift from blame to reflection.

> **66** I've been writing to Betsy, my imaginary pen pal for weeks now, and it really helps release the pressure. The other day, Jeanine said something that really hurt my feelings. When I got home, I wrote a letter to Betsy. Making up a person seemed weird at first, but it's actually helpful to write to "someone" that I don't feel like I have to justify myself to. I can just write it all down without worrying about what they're thinking.
> I'm not the best writer in the world, but who cares. I have an entire shoebox of letters now. I keep the box in my closet and every once in a while, I read a couple of them. Sometimes I even laugh at how serious I thought the situation was when I wrote to Betsy.
> —Emma **99**

Pretend you're writing to an imaginary pen pal: someone who really gets you. You trust this friend and are comfortable sharing your deepest thoughts and feelings with this person. Don't worry about grammar or spelling or penmanship. Only you will see the letter. Just get it out as quickly as you can. After you finish the letter, place it in an envelope and put it away for a few months. When you read it later, you may be surprised how different you feel.

You might try writing down your thoughts and feelings every couple of days or once a week so they're not bottled up for too long. The life of a teen isn't easy. Writing letters to an imaginary pen pal gets things that are bugging you out of your head and onto paper. This releases the pressure that fuels the drumbeat of anger.

Schedule Drum Practice

If you beat the anger drum, you may have noticed that the longer you beat it, the more difficult it is to stop. Pretty soon you're ruminating non-stop. Over time it becomes nearly impossible to stop. One thing that can help break the escalation of anger is to postpone anger rumination periods to a specific time—schedule "drum practice"! Limiting drum practice rather than trying to stop it once it starts is a bit easier and gives you more anger-free time. Also, scheduling anger drum practice weakens the habit your mind has developed to dwell on past hurts or slights. During the scheduled drum practice periods, you can use other tools you've just learned, such as watching or journaling.

SCHEDULE DRUM PRACTICE

1. Schedule drum practice 3–4 times every day for several weeks. Put the practice times in your calendar. Start with 5–10 minute practice sessions. Don't schedule drum practice just before bed. Also, don't schedule drum practice when you're in the situation that triggered the anger, such as when having lunch at school where the friend who triggered the anger hangs out too.

2. As soon as you notice that you're thinking about the anger-provoking situation, postpone drum practice to the nearest scheduled practice time. Say to yourself, "I'll think about that at my next practice session." Each time you begin to think about the situation, postpone the drum practice to the next session. You might do this many times between one practice session and the next. Don't give up. It takes time to break a thinking habit.

3. During the 5–10 minute practice session, use some of the tools you've learned. For example, write down all the anger thoughts, or watch the anger using the body scan meditation you learned. Don't distract yourself during the practice session. That's a great tool to use between practice sessions. Instead, say to yourself, "This is my drum beat time-and I can beat the drum as much as I like for the next few minutes."

4. With practice, it becomes easier to delay the mental drum beats until the scheduled times. You can then eliminate one of the drum practice sessions or shorten them a few minutes.

5. At the end of the week, set aside a few minutes to read your journal of anger thoughts. Does the situation feel any different? Do the anger thoughts feel less intense? Do you recognize any of the common thinking traps that you've learned?

Laugh a Little

Laughter and humor are great antidotes for difficult situations or emotions, even anger. It's tough to ruminate on a past hurt or slight while you're laughing. A good laugh turns anger on its head. There are many pluses to laughing rather than fuming:

> The other day my mom told me to rinse the breakfast dishes and put them in the dishwasher. I didn't want to do it. I was watching a show and who cares about a few dirty dishes in the sink? I told her that I would do it later. She said okay, but every ten minutes or so, she reminded me. After the third reminder, I yelled 'okay,' stormed into the kitchen and turned on the faucet full blast. The stream of water hit a plate and shot right into my face. I stood there for a minute soaked and covered with scrambled eggs and pieces of toast. I couldn't help it; I laughed. It was like something straight out of a sitcom. And when I laughed, my anger pretty much disappeared. When mom saw me laughing, wet and covered with breakfast, she started to laugh too.
> —Camila

- Anger stresses you while laughter relaxes you.
- Anger pushes people away while laughter draws people to you.
- Anger makes you focus on the situation while laughter helps you forget and move on.
- Anger brings you down while laughter makes you feel better.

LAUGHING OR FUMING

Instructions: Take a look at the following situations and see if you can come up with a funny ending. Imagine that you're writing a comedy show and you're writing the funny ending.

Situation	Funny Ending
Bridget is fuming. Her best friend, Lisabeth, isn't texting her back. It's been hours and she hasn't responded—what could she possibly be doing that's so important? Is she ignoring her?	Bridget usually calls Lisabeth "Lis," but since she's angry she types out her full name...only her phone autocorrects it to "Loss Beth." Bridget can't help but laugh—it's like her phone knows Lisabeth isn't there!
Jesus is fuming. As he was checking out a book from the public library, the librarian told him that he owed $20 in late charges. Jesus told the librarian that he didn't owe anything but the librarian kept telling him that he had to pay the fine.	
Amy is fuming. Her mom told her that she had to change into something "more appropriate" before she could go to the movie with friends.	
DeAndre is fuming. His math teacher told him to quiet down in class. DeAndre wasn't talking and said so. His math teacher didn't apologize and pretended that he didn't even hear him.	

Many situations that make you angry might be a little funny if you step back for a moment and look at it. You've probably had experiences when you're all set to fume and then you end up laughing a little.

Walk a Minute in Their Shoes

Anger gets in the way of understanding the hurt and pain of others. Someone does something that hurts or upsets you and a grudge forms as the drumbeat of anger beats and beats. As you ruminate, your anger builds into a throbbing ball of anger and resentment. That's when you lose your compassion for others and it becomes just about your hurt and their wrong. Trying to

WALK A MINUTE IN THEIR SHOES

1. Find a quiet and comfortable place. Sit or lie and close your eyes.
2. Permit your mind to go to the person and to the conflict you're having.
3. Accept that this is a difficult situation and how you're feeling about the person and the conflict. Hold onto these feelings for a moment or two but then let go of them. Imagine setting your feelings aside for a moment to make space for understanding and kindness.
4. Now, imagine how the situation feels and looks from the other person's perspective. Consider the situation that upsets you as part of the larger fabric of the other person's life. What is difficult for this person? What frightens and hurts this person?
5. Continue to imagine what life is like for the other person. What would it be like to walk in this person's shoes for a minute? What would it feel like to have the other person's life rather than yours for a day?
6. Finish this walk with a wish to you and the other person. Wish that you both can be happy and free from difficulties and suffering.

understand where the other person is coming from and, more importantly, seeing that they suffer too, is a balm that can soothe the anger you feel.

> I hate it when Calvin is late. I've asked him at least a hundred times to arrive on time. He just can't do it. But I'm tired of beating the anger drum so I decided that I'd walk a minute in his shoes, just to see what that was like. It was a tough minute. Calvin isn't just late with me. He's late with everyone, and he takes a lot of grief for it. I know he can't help it. He forgets things a lot. He forgets his homework, he loses his books, and his backpack. His teachers are on him all the time and so are his parents. He got kicked off the soccer team because he kept forgetting about practice, and Calvin loves soccer. I know that really sucks for him. After a minute, I felt less angry. I started to feel sympathy for him instead.
> —Jamal

Savor the Good and Pleasant

Savoring means enjoying a pleasant experience, such as savoring the taste and smell of a warm chocolate chip cookie. You can savor memories too, particularly memories of feeling happy or comfortable, such as the time you won a soccer game or even the taste of a slice of warm apple pie. Savoring a memory is another great tool to stop the drumbeat of anger. Savoring good and pleasant things interrupts the drumbeat and gives your mind time to relax. Savoring also creates pleasant feelings that combat the stress and worry that start anger outbursts.

SAVOR THE GOOD AND PLEASANT

Instructions: Savoring good and pleasant memories works best when you try to remember everything about the memory. Where were you? When did it happen? Who were you with? How did you feel?

1. First, think of three good times you had recently (e.g., favorite activities, favorite places you've visited, good times you've shared with friends or family, successes in your life).
2. Now, pick one of the good times and picture it in your mind. Then, write about it. Include the following: *Describe where you were and what was happening. What did you hear, smell, and see? Describe the good feelings that you felt (e.g., happy, proud, satisfied, joyful, loved). Describe the thoughts that were going through your mind when you were feeling the good feelings. Describe your role in making this good time happen. Did you set it up, or help make it happen? Imagine that this good time might lead to more good times and good feelings in the future. Describe what you imagine could happen in the future.*
3. Now that you've written about your good time and good feelings, read through it again. Finally, close your eyes and savor your good time by replaying it in your mind.
4. Rate the intensity of the image and the intensity of the good feelings you feel on a scale from 1 to 5, where 5 means the image or good feeling is very intense.
5. Last, savor the good and pleasant to interrupt the drum beat of anger. Practice savoring for 2 minutes and then checking for the drum beat. If it's still beating, savor for another 2 minutes. Keep going until the drum beat quiets.

Find the Good Thing in Someone

When we're angry, we tend to have trouble seeing the entire picture, particularly when it comes to people who upset or hurt us. We can only see the bad in the person. Tunnel vision like this keeps the anger beating until a hardened grudge forms. We keep thinking and re-thinking about the bad and upsetting thing the person did. Pretty soon the person gets the label "bad" in our heads. But very few people are really all bad. Most people have at least one good thing about them. Searching for and finding a good thing in someone, even if it's a very small thing, can slow the drumbeat of anger and soften resentment. That means you suffer less. To help you search, consider what other people see in the person. Perhaps the person:

- Has a small skill or accomplishment.
- Is kind to a friend or sibling.
- Takes care of a pet.
- Volunteers for a good cause.
- Smiles or says hello to you sometimes.

Practice Caring and Compassion Toward Yourself

Sometimes you might be angry with yourself for a mistake you made. Sometimes you might be angry with yourself for being angry with a friend, a parent, or a teacher you like. This anger might have hardened into a grudge against yourself for a mistake, or a misspoken word or action. You might call yourself names, think "I'm such an idiot," or hate yourself, and on and on the drum beats.

> The other day, I started to complain to my favorite teacher, Mr. Allen, about Juana. I was telling him that Juana is selfish and doesn't think about anyone but herself. I went on and on for a while. Mr. Allen just listened, and then said, "Juana isn't all bad." At first, I was angry that he was defending her, but then I realized that he was right. Of course she isn't ALL bad. And I guess I was never really trying to say she was. There are some things about her that annoy me, but she's fun and loves animals like I do. When I started to think about the good things about her, my drumbeat started to slow.
>
> —Ayanna

You may not be able to change the situation, or what you did or did not do, or change the people who hurt you. But you can change how you treat yourself. If this happens to you, showing a little care and compassion toward yourself can help slow the drumbeat of anger. To start, try repeating aloud or to yourself the following caring phrases when you begin to resent or dislike yourself:

- You're safe.
- You're good.
- You're okay.
- You deserve to be happy.
- You deserve to let this go.

Next, record and listen to the following loving-kindness meditation. As you listen to the meditation, allow the angry thoughts toward yourself to come out of the shadows. Permit them to come and then to go. Remind yourself that angry self-critical thoughts occur because you're scared, because you're hurt, and because you're in pain.

PRACTICE CARING AND COMPASSION

Instructions: In this meditation, you'll gather loving-kindness. We all have within us a natural capacity for loving-kindness. Loving-kindness is a friendship that's unconditional, that's open, gentle, and support-ive. Loving-kindness is a natural opening of a compassionate heart: to yourself and to others. It's a wish that you and everyone will be safe and happy. Record this script and listen to it every night at bedtime. Give it a try!

1.   Become comfortable in your chair or on your bed. Allow your hands to rest comfortably in your lap or on your stomach. Gently close your eyes.

2.   Become aware of the body and the breath. Feel your body and open yourself to whatever you're feeling in your body in this moment. Connect to the breath. Notice the wave-like movements of the belly.

3.   Begin with developing loving-kindness toward yourself. Allow your heart to open with tenderness. Allow yourself to open to your basic goodness. You might remember times you have been kind or generous. You might recall your natural desire to be happy and not to suffer. If acknowledging your own goodness is difficult, look at yourself through the eyes of someone who loves you. What does that person love about you?

4. As you experience this love, notice how you feel in your body. Maybe you feel some warmth in the face. Perhaps you feel a smile form at the corners of your mouth. This is loving-kindness, a natural feeling that all of us can have. Rest with this feeling of open, un-conditional love for a few minutes.

5. Breathe in the loving-kindness and breathe out again. Invite feelings of peace and acceptance into your life. Begin now to wish yourself well and extend words of loving-kindness to yourself.

6. And now, offer in your mind these words to yourself:

    • May I be filled with loving-kindness.

    • May I be held in loving-kindness.

    • May I feel connected and calm.

    • May I accept myself just as I am.

    • May I be happy.

    • May I know the natural joy of being alive.

7. And, now repeat in your mind these words of friendship and kind-ness to yourself once again:

    • May I be filled with loving-kindness.

    • May I be held in loving-kindness.

    • May I feel connected and calm.

    • May I accept myself just as I am.

    • May I be happy.

    • May I know the natural joy of being alive.

8.   Now you can open the circle of loving-kindness by bringing to mind someone who is dear to you. Someone whom you care about and who has always been supportive of you. Reflect on this person's basic goodness. Sense what you love about them. In your heart, feel your appreciation for this dear one, and begin your simple offering:

- May you be filled with loving-kindness.

- May you be held in loving-kindness.

- May you feel my love now.

- May you accept yourself just as you are.

- May you be happy.

- May you know the natural joy of being alive.

9.   Now bring to mind a "neutral" person. This is someone you might see regularly but don't know well. It might be a neighbor, a grocery store clerk, or a kid you see around school. Bring this person to mind now, and repeat the words of loving-kindness:

- May you be filled with loving-kindness.

- May you be held in loving-kindness.

- May you feel my love now.

- May you accept yourself just as you are.

- May you be happy.

- May you know the natural joy of being alive.

10.   And now, if it's possible for you, bring to mind someone with
       whom you've had a difficult relationship. Perhaps it's someone
       you don't like. Perhaps it's difficult for you to feel sympathy or
       compassion for this person. See if it's possible to let go of feelings
       of resentment and dislike for this person. Remind yourself to see
       this person as a whole being who deserves love and kindness. As
       someone who feels pain, hurt, fear, and anger too. Someone who
       also suffers. See if it's possible to extend to this person the words of
       loving-kindness in your mind:

       • May you be filled with loving-kindness.

       • May you be held in loving-kindness.

       • May you feel my love now.

       • May you accept yourself just as you are.

       • May you be happy.

       • May you know the natural joy of being alive.
       Now, allow your awareness to open in all directions: yourself,
       a dear one, a neutral person and a difficult person. Allow your
       awareness to open to all beings: humans and animals living every-
       where. Aware of all the joys and sorrows that all beings experi-
       ence, again think:

       • May all beings be filled with loving-kindness.

       • May all beings be happy.

       • May all beings awaken and be free.

       • May all beings know the natural joy of being alive.

       And now, bring this meditation to a close by coming back to ex-
       tend kindness to yourself. Rest for a while and bask in the energy
       of loving-kindness that may have been generated here.

> " I decided to try the loving-kindness meditation. I thought it was kind of silly, but I realized that I'm pretty hard on myself. My friends and parents tell me this all the time. I decided I would just try the meditation once in my room when no one else was in the house. I was a little embarrassed at first but then I kind of got into it. I felt relaxed by the end. The next day, I practiced the short phrases. I especially like, "You deserve to let this go." I said that phrase softly every time I felt frustrated with myself or anyone else. I also noticed that some of my friends are kind of hard on themselves too. So is my mom. I started to say it to them—I thought maybe they would laugh at me, but I think they actually appreciated it. My mom even said, "You're right. I deserve to let this go," and she did.
>
> —Jason "

Forgive

Forgiveness may feel impossible to use, particularly when you're beating the anger drum. As you've learned, anger tells you something is wrong. Perhaps someone has criticized you or put you down. Perhaps someone has hurt you and they don't even know it. When this happens, the drumbeat of anger starts and, over time, the anger builds and you become bitter. You form a serious grudge. Forgiveness is an antidote for lasting feelings of anger, bitterness, and revenge, particularly when there is nothing you can do to change the person or the situation.

What Is Forgiveness?

To forgive is to decide to let go of resentment and thoughts of revenge toward the person who hurt you. By forgiving, you're accepting what happened and finding a way to live with it. Forgiveness doesn't happen overnight. It's not easy for most people. Forgiveness takes time, and, for many, it's a gradual process.

How Can Forgiveness Help?

Let's get real. It's very difficult to forgive someone who wronged you. It might be the hardest thing you've ever done. But holding on to anger and resentment is hard to do, too. It takes a toll on you. Forgiveness, on the other hand, can:

- Stop the drumbeat of anger and lessen the grip that resentment has over you.
- Decrease your stress.
- Free you to move on and to mend relationships, and connect with others, if that is what you wish to do.
- Decreases the likelihood you will act on revenge.

Forgiveness is for you. Forgiving doesn't even need to include the person who wronged you. Most times, people won't even know you've forgiven them. Forgiveness isn't something you do for the person who wronged you. It's something you do for you.

If forgiveness helps us so much, why is it so difficult to do? Well, it's because most people don't understand what forgiveness is and what it is not.

Forgiveness does not mean that:

You must excuse the person's actions.

You must stop feeling hurt or upset about what happened.

You must forget what happened.

You must tell the person you forgive them.

You must include the person in your life.

You forgive in order to help the person who hurt you.

Four Steps of Forgiveness

Forgiveness begins with a recognition of your suffering and a willingness to make things better for yourself. Forgiveness is an ongoing action you take in response to the drumbeat of anger and resentment toward another person. Although forgiveness is difficult, maintaining anger and resentment is difficult too. Remember, forgiveness is for you and you deserve to be free of the drumbeat of resentment. If you decide you're willing to forgive, follow these four steps:

FOUR STEPS TO FORGIVENESS

Instructions: Find a quiet and comfortable place to be alone with your thoughts.

STEP 1: Accept the event and how it affected you: Think about the event that hurt you. Open yourself to the hurt and anger and accept how you feel about the event and the person who hurt you. Remind yourself that you may not get what you want even though you are a good person. Acknowledge that you might, in fact, get something better or worse than what you want. For example, "Even though I wanted Gloria to like me, I understand and accept that she might not like me and that doesn't make me or her a bad person."

STEP 2: *Acknowledge what you had hoped for and what you learned:* Acknowledge and accept that with every hurt there is something for you to learn if you are open to learning it. What did you learn about yourself that can help you grow from the event? Is this new knowledge useful to you? Is the lesson learned worth the hurt if you can use this new knowledge in the future? Decide (and it *is* a decision) to reconnect with your big dreams and your deepest hopes. Acknowledge that the hurt is part of your growth and development as a person. For example, "I have learned to be a better friend and this new knowledge will help me be the best friend I can to my other friends."

STEP 3: *Make room for understanding:* Now, think about the other person. That person is flawed and imperfect because all human beings are flawed and imperfect. Consider that the person may have acted without understanding the effects on you, or from the belief that their actions are okay or that the circumstance makes the action okay. Remind yourself that at times we all act from our limited understanding. Perhaps the person hurt you because the person needed something from you or from someone else. What do you think the person needed? Why did the person go after that need in a way that hurt you? For example, "This person is unable to see the good in me and others. This is her limitation."

STEP 4: *Take the long view:* Acknowledge the importance of practicing forgiveness every day. Remind yourself that forgiveness is a process and that each day presents opportunities to practice forgiveness with this grudge and then the next one. Since you may slip back into your old pattern of holding a grudge, ask a trusted friend or family member to remind you to forgive. Find people who have successfully forgiven others and listen to what they have to say. At times, you won't be able to set aside the resentment. Go ahead and give yourself permission to mull over the grudge for a short period—perhaps 15 minutes—then move on with your life. For example, "I decide today to learn all that I can to heal from this hurt and to move ahead with my life."

> **"** For days, all I could think about was what Mrs. Jameson, my social studies teacher, said to me and how unfair it was. The drum of anger kept beating, night and day, over and over. I realized that holding on to the anger was exhausting me. I wasn't sleeping. I wasn't eating. I just kept thinking of Mrs. Jameson and what she said. I was terrified that I would lose it at school and say something to her that would get me in big trouble. The crazy thing is that I know she isn't even thinking about any of this—today she smiled and waved at me! I decided that I would start to forgive Mrs. Jameson. It's not easy, I know it'll take some time, but it's helping me. I'm already feeling lighter and enjoying things more.
> —Alejandro **"**

IN A NUTSHELL

The drumbeat of anger drives your anger. Repeatedly thinking about a wrong or a slight intensifies anger and increases the likelihood you'll act before you think. Learning to stop the drumbeat of anger isn't easy but the tools in this chapter can help.

1. The easiest tool to use is distraction. When you notice your anger growing, distract yourself with an interesting or fun activity. Not only will the activity distract you from anger-evoking thoughts, it's likely more fun than beating the anger drum.

2. Even if you can't stop the drumming, you can contain it. Try scheduling practice. It really works.

3. Caring, compassion, and forgiveness aren't easy to practice, but they're great tools to stop the drumbeat. Compassion toward others and yourself can dampen the anger and connect you to the good things in you and other people.

CHAPTER 6

Communicate Clearly

Human beings use language to solve problems. Knowing how to express yourself and talk calmly through a problem is usually the best way to find a solution. For some, zero-to-60 anger means acting without thinking, which often means doing or saying something that makes things worse. Communicating clearly can prevent the conflicts and misunderstandings that fuel anger and can also help you resolve conflicts and misunderstandings quickly and effectively.

In this chapter, you'll learn five important communication tools:

- Express Anger Effectively.
- Listen Actively.
- Stand Up for Yourself.
- Take Feedback Effectively.
- Negotiate a Compromise.

Although learning to communicate clearly will take some time and practice, once you learn these tools, you'll use them in many situations beyond those that fuel anger. Tools to communicate clearly are life tools. You'll use these tools every day for the rest of your life to be happy and successful.

Express Anger Effectively

If you're a fan of history, you may have learned about Nikita Khrushchev pounding his shoe on the desk during a speech at the General Assembly of the United Nations in New York in 1960. Khrushchev was the First Secretary of the Communist Party of the Soviet Union. In addition to pounding his shoe, he called the other speaker a jerk, a stooge, and a lackey, and demanded that he stop speaking. The United Nations Assembly President abruptly ended the meeting. Although Khrushchev was pleased with his performance, other members of his delegation were embarrassed, and members of the General Assembly were angry. This didn't make Khrushchev many friends around the world.

Poor communication habits can create conflict and make it nearly impossible to resolve it. If you have zero-to-60 anger, conflict fuels anger even more. Therefore, learning to communicate clearly, particularly when you're feeling a bit angry, is an important tool.

What You Call Anger Makes a Difference

The words we use to describe our experiences can affect the intensity of those experiences. Let's say you're waiting to get a vaccination and thinking about the pain of the injection. You might think, "The pain is going to be horrible," or "The pain is going to feel like a little splinter." Which description do you think will intensify the pain you feel? It's the same for anger. The words you use to express anger can heat up or cool down the anger you feel. Take a look at the words we use for anger and note the ones you think increase the intensity anger.

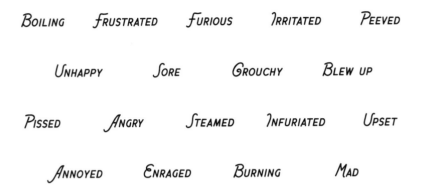

Boiling   Frustrated   Furious   Irritated   Peeved

Unhappy   Sore   Grouchy   Blew up

Pissed   Angry   Steamed   Infuriated   Upset

Annoyed   Enraged   Burning   Mad

You might not realize it, but strong words tend to cause strong anger. You probably use strong anger words automatically, even when the situation isn't that bad. That doesn't mean you can't learn to use calmer words. It just takes a little practice.

CAMILA'S COOL WORD PRACTICE

Situation	Hot Words	Cool Words
Julie didn't return my texts.	I'm boiling.	I'm bummed.
My teacher gave me a C.	I'm about to lose it.	I'm kind of upset.
A girl bumped into me and didn't say she was sorry.	I'm furious.	I'm annoyed.
A guy laughed at me.	I'm going ballistic.	I'm irritated.

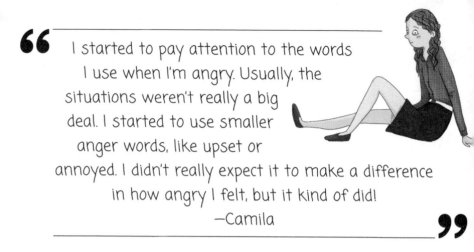

" I started to pay attention to the words I use when I'm angry. Usually, the situations weren't really a big deal. I started to use smaller anger words, like upset or annoyed. I didn't really expect it to make a difference in how angry I felt, but it kind of did!

—Camila "

Communicate Clearly With Your Body

If you watch a show with the sound turned off, you can probably tell which characters are angry just by the look on their faces. If you then close your eyes and turn the sound on, you can probably tell which characters are angry by the volume of their voices and the words they use. That's the way anger works, and you can use this understanding to cool your anger.

Our bodies send signals, too, and our feelings often follow our bodies. When someone smiles at us, we smile back. When we smile, we signal that we're calm, approachable, and open to listening to what someone wants to say. When we frown, we signal that we're upset, that others should back off, and that we're not particularly open to listening to the other person. We tend to read body signals in order to tell how someone is feeling. When someone frowns, we're likely to think they're angry or upset. A little smile, even a half of a smile, rather than a scowl, can make you seem more approachable and even change how you feel a little.

Communicating clearly with your body is important when you speak to people, when you assert yourself, or when you negotiate with someone, especially when you're working to resolve a conflict. Also, speaking clearly at a volume that's appropriate to the situation or environment is important. Like how if you're in the library, you use a quiet voice and not the packed basketball stadium voice.

THE 4 C'S OF COMMUNICATING CLEARLY WITH YOUR BODY

	What Not to Do	What to Do
Calm voice	Mumble. Shout or yell.	Speak calmly and at a volume suitable to the environment.
Calm body	Clench your fists, pace, or gesture harshly. Slouch. Point or threaten with your hands.	Try a half-smile. Stand tall. Face the person.
Connect with your eyes	Look down or away. Squint.	Maintain eye contact. Open your eyes and raise your eyebrows.
Create space	Get in the person's face. Lean in toward the person.	Keep an arm's length from the person. Lean back a little.

Communicate Clearly with Your Words

If a kid is kicking the back of your chair in class, it makes sense that you'd want him to stop. How you get him to stop is the key. A big part of solving a problem between you and someone else depends on how you speak to the person. Sometimes people don't know what to say when they're angry other than what they've heard others say when they're angry:

- Sarcasm: "Who made you queen of the universe?" "Yeah, because you're always right."
- Swear words.
- Put-downs: "You couldn't hit the ball if your life depended on it."
- Dismissive comments: "If you say so." "Whatever." "Yeah, right."

You can learn to use words that get your point across but don't fuel your anger. You might try these next time:

TAKE THE STING OUT OF ANGRY WORDS

I don't like that.	Stop it.
Leave me alone.	I'm angry because ...
Please don't do that.	Cut it out.
Knock it off.	Let's move on.

Use I-Messages

At the most basic level, we send either You-messages or I-messages, and You-messages can make communicating with someone, particularly during a conflict, much more difficult. You-messages put people on the defensive, particularly when you use words such as, "should," "must," "ought to," "need to," "always," and "never." When you say to a friend, "You should get this kind of soda, not that kind" it sounds as if you're telling him he's stupid for liking the soda he likes. When you tell a friend, "You never listen to me," it sounds as if you're attacking her. When you send a You-message, people stop listening and wait for the attack.

I-messages, on the other hand, help you clearly and honestly express yourself without blaming others. When you send an I-message, you take responsibility for how you think and feel, which is less likely to put someone on the defensive. Even if the person isn't on the defensive, I-messages increase the likelihood you'll come to a solution that works for both of you. I-messages put people at ease because it sounds as if it's about you and not about them (even if it is about them). Using I-messages rather than You-messages improves your relationships with friends, family, and teachers. Better relationships mean less stress in your life.

An I-message includes three parts: **I feel ... when you ... because ....** With a little practice, you'll be sending I-messages regularly:

I-MESSAGES VERSUS YOU-MESSAGES

You're angry with your friend Amanda because she's been sitting on the bus with Amy all week and not speaking to you.

You-Message	**I-Message**
"You never sit and talk with me anymore."	"I feel hurt when you sit with Amy on the bus and ignore me because it makes me think that you don't want to be my friend anymore."

You are angry with your friend Alfonso because he shared his lunch with Tim and didn't offer you any.

You-Message	**I-Message**
"You should give your lunch to me because I'm your best friend, not Tim."	"I feel angry when you share your lunch with Tim without asking me if I want some because I think that you care more about Tim than me."

> At first, it felt weird to use I-messages. I was so used to telling my friends, "You should do this, or you should do that." It was automatic. But once I started to use I-messages, I noticed that my friends were responding better. They didn't get as defensive and would listen to me more. That helped a lot. We've been getting along better.
> —Alejandro

Avoid Mixed Signals

One last word about expressing anger effectively: make certain you don't send mixed signals. It's important your words and body match. You want to signal to the other person that you're calm and open, so use a neutral facial expression rather than a scowl. Even better, try a half-smile and raise your eyebrows slightly. You might want to practice in front of a mirror. First, squint your eyes and scowl and say "Bubble." How does that look? Next, smile, raise your eyebrows and say "Bubble." Try this with other phrases, such as "Have a great day," or "Nice to meet you." Matching your body to your words is very important if you want to avoid sending the wrong signal. A mismatch between your words and your body can sound sarcastic or like you don't really mean what you're saying.

Listen Actively

There's hearing and then there's listening, and listening takes a lot more work. Arguments, conflicts, and anger often occur because people aren't listening to each other. When you know how to actively listen, you can prevent misunderstandings and work through them effectively when they do happen. Listening actively builds strong connections to people. The more solid the connections to friends and family members, the less likely misunderstandings will damage the relationships. Strong connections make life easier and protect your friendships from the occasional misunderstanding. To listen actively, follow these three steps:

- **Listen** carefully to what the person is saying.
- **Repeat** what the person said back to them.
- **Clarify** the point or problem the person is making.

Listen Carefully

Anger makes listening, not hearing, difficult because we're not paying attention to what the other person is saying. We're caught up in the drumbeat of anger, or we're thinking of a comeback or counterargument. At the same time, we're working hard to remain cool. That takes attention too. Anger makes it hard to pay attention, and it's necessary to pay attention in order to listen to what the other person is saying. When you learn to actively listen, it'll not only help you to pay attention, but you'll actually understand what they're saying and where they're coming from.

Repeat It Back

Anger often results from reacting to what you think a person said without knowing for certain that is indeed what the person said (or meant). You can easily avoid these misunderstandings when you repeat back what the person said to you. In order repeat back what you heard correctly, it's necessary to listen carefully.

You can repeat back what the person said in two ways. You can repeat exactly what the person said, or you can reword it.

When you reword, you don't repeat back the same words like a parrot. Instead, you repeat an approximation of what the person said. Here are a couple of examples of repeating and rewording:

REPEAT IN ORDER TO LISTEN CAREFULLY

What Speaker Says	What You Say
It's really hot today.	*Repeat:* It's really hot today. *Paraphrase:* It's boiling today.
I'm ahead of you in line.	*Repeat:* You're ahead of me in line. *Paraphrase:* You're in front of me.
Give my book back.	*Repeat:* You want your book back. *Paraphrase:* You want me to return your book.
Can I borrow your soccer ball today?	*Repeat:* You want to borrow my soccer ball today. *Paraphrase:* You want to use my soccer ball today.

Clarify the Point or Problem

Misinterpretation or jumping to the wrong conclusion often results in hurt feelings, anger, and needless arguments. Clarifying or checking your assumptions about the point or problem helps you check that you have the correct information before you react. You'll then know you and the other person are talking about the same thing, even if you have different opinions about it. Once you accurately understand the problem, you can use the problem-solving tool you'll learn in the next chapter to solve it. Even when you understand or you're pretty certain you understand, clarifying shows the other party that you're listening, which can't hurt.

> 66
>
> The clarifying tool saved me from a big argument with my best friend, Jasmine. Yesterday, we were walking home together. She was texting one of our friends while we were talking to each other. When we got to my house, I asked her if she wanted to go to a movie with me on Saturday. She said, "Sure," and started to walk away. I thought maybe she was distracted, so I checked with her, just in case: "Okay, so noon on Saturday?" Jasmine stopped and said, "Oh no, I thought you said Sunday. It's my grandmother's birthday on Saturday, and we're getting together to celebrate. I'm sorry. How about Sunday?" If I hadn't taken two seconds to check this out with her, she would have (accidentally) stood me up and I would have been angry for sure.
>
> —Ayanna
>
> 99

Like most things, it takes practice to get good at listening actively. A great way to practice is with a close friend. The next time you're hanging out, ask your friend a question. Then, practice listening actively. What did you notice?

Stand Up for Yourself

Sometimes a kid teases you. Sometimes a friend borrows your things and then breaks or loses them. Sometimes your parents tell you that you can go out with friends but then change their minds. Sometimes a teacher gives you a low grade you don't deserve or thinks you did something wrong when you didn't. At these times, it's important to stand up for yourself.

WHEN STANDING UP FOR YOURSELF MAKES SENSE	
Friends pushing you to skip class.	Friends asking you to do their homework.
Parents asking you to do a chore while you're in the middle of something else important.	Teachers asking you to do extra work without a good reason.
Friends pushing you to take sides.	Coaches pushing you to work harder when you're already working at the max.
Adults pushing you to do something that doesn't make sense to you.	Friends pushing you to do drugs.
Friends teasing you.	Teachers telling you to be quiet when you weren't talking.

You Have Rights Too

You have the right to be treated with respect and to stand up for your rights. There are two ways to stand up for yourself. You could use anger to get people to back down. Or, you can stand up for yourself in a respectful, calm manner and assert your rights without hurting another person's feelings or stepping on *their* rights. We all feel angry when we're treated unfairly or when our rights are ignored. Perhaps others treat you unfairly because you're not an adult. Still, even teens have rights. You have the right to respect, safety, privacy, and to be listened to.

Passive, Aggressive, or Assertive

There are three ways to handle conflicts or situations. There's the *passive* way, when you let someone take away your rights and you don't do anything to stop them. There is the *aggressive* way, when you get angry, demand your rights, and do not consider the feelings and rights of the other person. Then, there is the in between or *assertive* way, when you stand up for your rights calmly and clearly but respect the feelings and rights of the other person.

Assertiveness is the best way to respond to conflict because it doesn't usually escalate it. Neither acting aggressively nor passively is likely to get you what you want. If you act aggressively, people will either walk away or get in your face. If you act passively, people won't even know that you want something. Sometimes, even acting assertively won't get you what you want—but it will give you the best shot.

The assertive way covers a lot of territory. Assertiveness can include giving feedback to a friend when he repeatedly arrives late or doesn't keep other commitments to you. Assertiveness can include giving feedback to a sister about borrowing your things without asking. The assertive way can also include (and this is much more difficult to do) giving feedback to a teacher about the grade they gave you or to a parent who sets an unreasonable curfew for you.

In other words, assertiveness means you're willing to stand up for yourself and to ask and expect to be treated fairly. It means you're willing to state what you believe in and what you want to do and don't want to do. The assertive way can include asking for a ride, or for permission to stay out a bit later than usual. It can include saying no to an unreasonable request from someone, such a friend who wants to copy your homework or borrow your favorite sweater. It can include demands that others stop doing something, such as stop teasing you, or requests to start doing something, such as politely asking someone to move so you can get through the doorway.

PASSIVE, AGGRESSIVE, OR ASSERTIVE

Passive	You hold in your feelings rather than expressing them. You might not stand up for yourself because you're afraid that you'll hurt someone's feelings by telling them how you feel, whether it's that you're feeling hurt, disappointed, or even worried. You may want to get along so much that you put your wishes or your rights on the back burner; or, you might feel guilty about asking for what you want even when others seem not to have problems doing this. However, the passive way of handling situations tends to backfire. Rather than telling them how you feel, you expect them to figure out what you want without you telling them. When they don't figure it out, you might feel hurt and then angry.
Aggressive	You express what you want or don't want in a hostile way. You might threaten people or intimidate them, even without knowing it. You might call them names, or ridicule them. You might insist that you're "right" and demand that you get your way. However, although the aggressive way might get you what you want sometimes, it creates more problems for you in the long run. You can lose friends and end up with what you want but no one to enjoy it with.

Assertive You express your wants and wishes calmly, politely, and honestly while you respect the rights and feelings of others. You take the guess work out of your interactions with people because they know where you're coming from. At the same time, the assertive way makes you a great listener, and signals to people that you're open to working things out.

PASSIVE, AGGRESSIVE, AND ASSERTIVE RESPONSES TO SITUATIONS

Situation: *A kid takes your phone without asking and you want it back.*

Passive	Aggressive	Assertive
"Please don't break my phone."	"Give back my phone you jerk!"	"Give back my phone."

Situation: *A kid keeps kicking the back of your chair after you asked him to stop.*

Passive	Aggressive	Assertive
"It's okay. I can move."	"You moron. If you kick my chair one more time I'll kill you!"	"If you don't stop kicking my chair, I'm going tell the teacher."

Situation: *Your mom asks you to clean your room when you're in the middle of texting a friend.*

Passive	Aggressive	Assertive
Walk away and keep texting friend.	"You're such a control freak! You can't leave me alone for even a second."	"Mom, please give me five minutes to finish this text and then I'll clean my room. Is that okay?"

DEAL to Stand Up for Yourself

It takes a lot of skill to stand up for yourself, particularly with people who have more power than you, such as teachers and parents. At those times, the anger might cloud your thinking, and you might act before you think, so it helps to follow a few simple steps to stand up for yourself and DEAL with the situation. DEAL stands for **D**escribe, **E**xpress, **A**sk, and **L**ist. DEAL can help you stand up for yourself, ask for help, and manage conflicts. It's important to follow these steps in a calm and respectful way, without being aggressive or pushy. Remember to send the right signal with a calm voice, calm body, and calm words!

DEAL TO STAND UP FOR YOURSELF

1. **Describe** the problem. When you're talking to someone, tell them what the problem is. For example, "This is the third time you told me you would help me with my homework but you keep bailing out at the last minute."

2. **Express** how the problem is making you feel. After you have described the problem, express how it makes you feel but without blaming the other person. For example, "Once or twice is okay, but three times makes me think you don't care. It hurts my feelings."

3. **Ask** for a change. Once you have told them what the problem is and how it is making you feel, it is time to ask for some change, which you hope will fix the problem. Suggest a solution. "I completely understand that sometimes you're too busy to help me. That's fine! But if you think that's going to be the case, please don't tell me you'll be able to. I'd rather know in advance."

4. **List** how you think the change is going to improve your situation, or fix the problem. This will motivate the person to try out your idea. For example, "I think that if you tell me straight up that you can't help me, then I'll know that I need to get some help from someone else, and I won't be stuck last minute."

If stress fuels your anger, assertiveness can help. This means you stand up for your right to do what is reasonable and to say no thank you to what is unreasonable. It is stressful when people add things to your plate if your plate is already full. Standing up for yourself and saying no can help you feel less overwhelmed and powerless when people ask you to do more when you're already doing a lot.

> **"** My plate is totally full this week. I have a big social studies exam to study for, and I need to spend more time working on my essay for English class. Also, it's my dad's birthday, and my mom asked me to help her prep for the party. I was already feeling overwhelmed by the number of things on my plate and then Mr. Thomas, my favorite teacher, asked whether I would be willing to tutor a couple of his students in math this week. I didn't want to say no to Mr. Thomas—he's helped me a lot with my college applications! But I knew that saying no was the right thing to do and I used DEAL to do it. Mr. Thomas was totally cool with it and even thanked me for telling him that my plate was too full to take on a tutoring gig.
> —Jamal **"**

At times, you might not feel comfortable asserting yourself, such as when you're dealing with a teacher, coach, or older teen. In those situations, you might ask a friend or another adult to help you assert yourself, or at least pave the way.

> **"** My English teacher marked me down a grade because I turned in my paper late. When I went to her and explained that I had finished it on time, she wouldn't listen to me. I decided to ask my science teacher for help, since he had asked me to help him prepare for the big lab project that day. He came with me and helped me talk to my English teacher. Together, we fixed it, and I got full credit for the paper.
> —Ayanna **"**

Stand-Up Sandwich

Sometimes you'll want to package your assertive statement so it's a little more appetizing to the person. This is the stand-up sandwich. A sandwich is two slices of bread on either side of the main attraction (the stuff inside). It's not possible to use a stand-up sandwich every time, but it works great when you can. A stand-up sandwich includes a nice comment on either side of the assertive request. Beginning with something nice gets the person's attention. Ending with something nice makes it more difficult for them to say no to the assertive request. Here are a couple of examples:

"You make evolutionary biology so interesting even though it's complex."

"Could I please have an extension to completely analyze my results and prepare my final lab report?"

"I've learned a ton from you on this project. Just need a little more time to get it all done."

"You make cooking fun, Mom."

**"Okay if I have 5 minutes more online and then
help with dinner?"**

"Teamwork, right?"

The trick to the stand-up sandwich is to be honest and sincere. If you can't think of something nice to say that is true about the person, it's better just to ask for what you want calmly and politely.

Hit the Repeat Button

Sometimes people don't respond the first time you DEAL. Perhaps they didn't hear you or perhaps they're not accustomed to you standing up for yourself. Either way, don't give up too soon.

- "Please give me back my phone."
- "Give me back my phone now, please."
- "Please give me my phone."
- "I'd like you to give me my phone, please."

Keep repeating the assertive request. You can change it around a little, but keep repeating the request in a calm, clear, polite, and direct way until the person agrees or walks away.

Take Feedback Effectively

Often anger and conflict erupt when someone doesn't take well-meaning feedback well. There can be several reasons for this, like assuming the person is trying to put you down or blame you for something. You learned about changing these hot anger thoughts in Chapter 4. Here are a couple of other simple tools to help you take feedback without getting angry.

Fog the Feedback

Fogging is a simple tool that helps you accept feedback calmly without feeling frustrated or angry. The idea is that you're like a thick, dense fog that absorbs and then hides harsh feedback. When someone throws a stone at you, the stone sinks into your fog and slows down. Practically, this means you absorb the feedback, but instead of responding with defensiveness and anger, you just state back the facts, but don't react to opinion-based criticisms. Once you fog the feedback, you're less likely to throw the stone back at the person because the feedback doesn't feel as harsh. And when you don't respond with defensiveness and anger, the other person is unlikely to keep being aggressive. This technique is amazingly practical, easy to learn, and works great when someone is giving you overly critical feedback. Rather than steaming, try fogging.

66

I tried this with my dad. He's not the best communicator in the world. Last night, I asked him for help with my essay. He started to go on and on about the topic and how I hadn't organized the material clearly. I knew he was trying to help but I started to get annoyed. So I imagined that I was sitting in a cloud of fog. Every time he said something, I imagined his words coming at me, entering the fog, and slowing down. I even imagined his words absorbing some of the fog and puffing up and then disappearing. Fogging his critical feedback made it a lot easier for me to take in his actual suggestions (which, fine, weren't that bad).

—Jason

99

See the Forest and the Tree

Sometimes teens only hear the criticism or the single thing the person would like them to do differently next time. They don't hear or take in the many positive things in the feedback. This is a bit like over-focusing on a tree and missing that you're surrounded by a forest. When your attention locks on the negative, try listening for the good things. Practice listening actively. Repeat back to the person the compliments and good things you hear: "You like that I'm always on time," or, "You're pleased with the way I straightened my closet." Listening actively can help you step back and take in all the feedback: the positive and the negative.

Take It in

Often, when someone is giving us feedback, we're not really listening. We're certainly not listening in the active way you learned earlier in this chapter. We're thinking of comebacks or arguments to what the person is saying, all the while failing to hear what someone really means. This can cause us to misunderstand and jump to incorrect conclusions, fueling anger and conflict. If you find yourself thinking through what you're going to say next, start to listen actively. Repeat back and clarify what you hear. Also, watch what the person's body is signaling. Is the person calm, smiling, and relaxed? If yes, then this is likely caring feedback, not critical feedback.

Thank the Person

Thanking the person for the feedback signals to them that you've heard what the person said to you and that you're open to learning from it. Thanking the person for feedback is the opposite of being defensive, and the person will get that. Thanking them for the feedback doesn't mean they're right and you're wrong. Nor does it mean you agree with the feedback and you must act on it. It just means you took in what the person said. Remember, they cared enough about this and about you to mention it to you.

Negotiate a Compromise

Another great anger-busting tool is negotiation. Negotiating means you and another person work to find a compromise to a situation. When you and the person reach a compromise, each of you wins a little and loses a little, and that way, you both win. Negotiating a compromise can prevent future disagreements or conflicts about a situation because everyone involved feels like they've gotten something and given something back.

Because people are different, they often have different solutions to a problem. Therefore, it's important to consider not only what you want and how you will say it but also the effect of what you want and say on the other person. Will your suggestion solve the problem or make it worse? Will making your request improve your relationship with the person or damage it? The best negotiations begin before you even meet and speak with the person. A little preparation pays big time when negotiating a compromise:

NEGOTIATE A COMPROMISE

1. Make a T-chart by drawing two columns on the page.
2. At the top of the left column, write "Where I Could Give in A Little" and then write the things about the situation where you could give in a little.
3. Next, at the top of the right column, write "Where I Hold Firm" and list those things you want to stay firm on.
4. Then try to find a middle ground. Use your two-column idea list to find someplace in between your ideas that might serve as a compromise. Being a negotiator means thinking carefully about both sides of the situation, and then making a decision that satisfies everyone.

5. Finally, meet face-to-face, and negotiate your compromise. Sometimes the first compromise doesn't work. Or, you realize that you have given in more than the other person and it doesn't feel good. If this is the case, go back to the T-chart and review your ideas. Then, let the other person know the first compromise didn't work for you and that you would like to try again.

During the negotiation, signal to the other person that you're open and there is a middle ground. Smile, nod your head as you listen, let them know you're happy to negotiate, and you'll be fair to the other person and fair to yourself.

> My parents are pretty strict about my curfew, but I want to stay out later on the weekends. The problem is my parents want me home by 9pm and I'm only allowed to go to my friends' houses. And they won't let me get a ride from another kid! Only adults. It seemed like the only way to get them to change a little was for me to compromise and change a little too. I thought about where I could give a little. I decided that if they would let me stay out later, I would agree to get a ride home from a friend's parent or call my dad for a ride. I also thought about what I wasn't willing to compromise on. I didn't want to only go to friends' houses—if I did that, there would be no-one to hang with, because they all get to go out! They surprised me and compromised a little on this one. We agreed that as long as I don't go into the city at night, I can go to the movies and other places in our town.
> —Emma

IN A NUTSHELL

The quickest way to provoke anger and a big argument is when people don't communicate clearly with each other.

1. Misunderstandings fuel anger. Listen actively to signal that you're not only hearing what the person is saying, but that you understand.

2. You have rights, and it's okay to stand up for yourself. Use DEAL to assert your rights calmly and clearly while also respecting the feelings and rights of the other person.

3. People have different solutions to problems because they see the problem differently. That doesn't mean you can't find a middle ground. Negotiate a compromise that feels good to you and to the other person. Compromises build relationships. Anger tears them down.

CHAPTER 7

Solve Problems

If you're like most people, you run into a problem now and then. A friend borrowed your game controller and forgot to return it to you. Your teacher yelled at you for talking in class, but it was the kid next to you doing the talking. Your dad said you couldn't hang out with friends until you cleaned your room. Truth be told, it's not like anger doesn't solve problems. If you blow up and tell off your friend, he might not keep you waiting again. If you're angry and say something sarcastic to the teacher, she might get the message and not falsely accuse you again. If you lose it and yell at your dad, you might convince him hanging out with friends is more important than cleaning your room. But solving problems with anger often creates more and bigger problems.

In this chapter, you'll learn a simple way to find solutions to problems. Because anger often clouds our thinking, it helps to have a simple set of steps you can do automatically. You'll also create solution packages for the typical problems that arise in your life.

These solution packages will help you calmly and quickly solve problems that provoke anger and frustration.

Get to the Solution Before Anger Gets to You

Anger signals that something is a problem and motivates you to find a solution. For example, in Chapter 4, Ayanna was angry about the dress code at her school. She thinks it's unfair that the school decides what's appropriate or inappropriate to wear and it's messing with her style, which is something that's very important to her. Ayanna's anger might motivate her to run for class president to change things, start a petition, or talk to her school principal. These are all great solutions to the problem of unfairness. However, if Ayanna gets too angry, she might shoot right past these reasonable solutions and fall into the trap of using anger to solve the problem of unfairness. She might scream at her teacher who politely reminds her of the dress code, she might dress over the top to make her point, or she might even refuse to attend classes until the school changes its policy. Although these are solutions, they're angry solutions that likely won't solve the problem and, worse yet, are certain to create more issues for Ayanna in the end.

Using anger to solve problems is often automatic. It's a mental program you follow without thinking. But just because solving problems with anger is automatic doesn't mean you can't learn another mental program that becomes automatic, too. It's like when you learned to ride a bicycle. Once you learned the mental bicycle-riding program, riding a bicycle became automatic. You can jump on any bicycle and ride away, without any effort or thought.

In this section, you'll learn a new mental program to solve problems that, with practice, will become automatic. Because anger can cloud your thinking, it helps to have a simple mental program to follow that guides you through the steps of effective problem solving. The ICCAN approach will help you break apart problems, make good choices, and create fewer problems for you. To use ICCAN, follow these five steps:

- **I**dentify the problem.
- **C**onsider solutions that might help.
- **C**onsider consequences of each choice.
- **A**pply a solution.
- **N**ow, review how the solution worked!

Identify the Problem

The first step is to identify the problem. Problems that involve other people are much more likely to lead to anger, arguments, and conflicts, so we'll focus on those situations. There is always more than one way to solve a people problem. When identifying the problem, you'll want to ask yourself four questions:

- What event or situation triggered the anger?
- What did you do?
- What did the other person do?
- What happened to you then?

Now, we'll break apart three situations that made Jason angry. Jason fell into the trap of using anger all three times to solve a problem, and each time bad things happened to him.

JASON'S ANGER SITUATIONS

What happened?	What did you do?	What did the other person do?	What happened to you then?
My dad told me I couldn't play basketball until I finished my homework.	I screamed at him and threw the basketball across the room and broke a lamp.	My dad got upset.	He made me pay for the lamp out of my allowance.
My brother ate the last slice of my birthday cake.	I threw the cake plate at him.	He told mom.	I had to go to my room and couldn't play my video game that day.
The bus driver told me to move my feet out of the aisle.	I ignored her and kept my feet in the aisle.	She told me that she wasn't going to move the bus until I moved my feet.	My friends were angry with me because they wanted to go home.

Consider Solutions That Might Help

The next step is to consider solutions (other than anger) to solve a problem. The solutions you use to solve most problems will include the skills you've learned so far, such as clear communication, assertiveness, negotiation, and strategies to calm your body and thoughts. Most of the solutions we use to solve problems, particularly when the problem is a disagreement or conflict with someone, are the same. We either ask someone for help, apologize, or negotiate. Sometimes it makes sense just to walk away.

After you identify the problem, brainstorm a list of potential solutions. It's best to come up with as many potential solutions as possible, no matter how silly they may be. Brainstorming is all about quantity, not quality, so don't throw away any potential

TYPICAL CHOICES OR SOLUTIONS TO PROBLEMS

Seek help   Ask a friend to help you.

Tell your teacher.

Ask your parents to help you.

Negotiate   Try to settle the problem.

Ask for what you want.

Explain what you want.

Apologize   Say that you're sorry when you made a mistake.

Say that you're sorry that the situation upset the person.

Angry words   Say something mean or hurtful.

Say something sarcastic.

Angry actions   Hit, kick, or push the person.

Fight with the person.

Avoid   Walk away from the situation.

Don't speak up but blow up later.

Refuse to do something or do something in a way that causes you more problems later.

solution when you brainstorm. You'll decide in the next step which solution is likely to be a good one or bad one. With some practice, you can find a solution that solves, manages, or at least improves most problems. Check out Jason's ICCAN form on the following page to see how he worked through each of the following steps for a problem with his dad. He did a great job of brainstorming potential solutions. He even came up with a silly one.

Consider Consequences of Each Choice

After you list all the potential solutions, the next step is to consider consequences for each solution. To make a good decision, it's best to think about all the possible consequences that might get you what you want and not make things worse for you or fuel conflict and anger. Remember, anger can go from zero to 60 in seconds. This doesn't give you much time to think through the consequences, and there are almost always consequences for zero-to-60 anger—even little ones. Here are several questions to help you think through the possible consequences of your actions on other people:

- How would the person feel if I did this?
- What might the person do if I did this?
- What else might happen?

As you practice thinking through possible consequences for each solution, you're building a new mental program that will automatically start when you run into a problem

Apply a Solution

Next, select one of the solutions and try it. The best solution is the one most likely to work and least likely to cause you more problems. There is seldom a perfect solution to a problem, but

JASON'S ICCAN FORM

What happened that triggered the anger?	Choices: What could you have done in the situation?	Consequences (for each choice)
My dad told me I couldn't shoot hoops until I finished my homework.	Ask mom to tell dad to let me shoot hoops before homework.	Mom always sides with dad. Mom tells dad and he gets upset and this guarantees no hoops tonight.
	Go on strike and refuse to do my homework tonight.	I get behind in math and get even more stressed.
	Rush through my homework so that I have time to shoot hoops.	I don't do well in school and then can't play on the school basketball team.
	Ask Dad if I can shoot hoops for 30 minutes and then promise to do an extra 30 minutes of homework.	He might consider this, since it gives him something he wants (me to do more homework).
	I scream at him and throw the basketball across the room.	My mom and dad get upset and ground me for the week.
	Ask my older sister to do my homework for me so that I can shoot hoops.	Fat chance!

What is best choice (solution) to this problem? Remember, the best choice is the one that's most likely to work and the least likely to cause you more problems.	I could have asked Dad if I can shoot hoops for 30 minutes and then promise to do an extra 30 minutes of homework. If he says no, I could promise to do an extra 45 minutes.

there are many good solutions that can help a little while not making things worse. You can't know whether a solution works until you try it.

Now Review How the Solution Worked

The final step in the problem-solving program is to take a look at how well the solution worked and praise yourself for sticking with the process. To help you decide how well a solution worked, imagine a target. If you hit the bullseye your solution worked great. This means you got what you wanted AND it didn't create other problems for you. Remember this! You'll want to include this solution when you build Hassle Plans to handle conflicts, arguments, and disagreements that occur between you and other people. You'll learn about those next.

If the solution hit the target but wasn't a bullseye, this means you'll want to modify the solution a little. For example, if Jason's solution to negotiate with his dad didn't work, he might offer to do a small job around the house next time in addition

> **❝** I used the ICCAN model to come up with a solution that might work with my dad. It sounds so simple, but when I stopped and made myself think about how he would react to each, the solution was suddenly obvious. It's not like my dad always says no to me—negotiating with him makes more sense than yelling at him.
> —Jason **❞**

to 30 minutes more of homework. Sometimes, adding a tool can also change a good solution into a bullseye choice. For example, Jason might try leading with an apology, "Dad, I know you want me to do well in school, and I do, too. I'm sorry that I'm falling behind in my schoolwork. I promise I'm going to work harder." Jason could then continue to negotiate with his dad.

If the solution missed the target completely, this means it didn't work at all or, worse yet, created more problems for you. Select another solution from the list or brainstorm more. Sometimes, trying one solution leads you to other solutions you didn't think of the first time you brainstormed.

IN A NUTSHELL

Problem solving is a great anger-busting tool, particularly when you think through all the solutions you have and the benefits, as well as the costs or consequences, of each solution.

1. The best solution for a problem with someone is the one most likely to work and least likely to make more problems for you later.

2. The solutions you use to solve a problem with someone are the ones you've learned, such as standing up for yourself, sending the right signal with your voice and body, and listening actively, to name just a few.

3. If you're too frustrated to think clearly through all the solutions and consequences when using the ICCAN tool, try your cool body and cool thoughts tools first. Then, when you're feeling calmer, go back to the ICCAN tool.

CHAPTER 8

Handle Accusations and Put-Downs

Accusations, both true and false, as well as teasing and put-downs, are an unfortunate part of everyone's life. These are the conflicts you might encounter at home, at school, with friends, teachers, parents, and siblings. For example, a teacher accuses you of cheating when you didn't, or your parents catch you lying—when you did. Or, a friend calls you a loser and you know she's joking, but another kid calls you a loser and you know he's not. As hard and hurtful as these conflicts are, you can learn to handle them before your anger gets out of control.

In this chapter, you'll first learn about the conflict steps. You can climb up the steps and increase the conflict by reacting in unhelpful ways to what the other person does and says. Or, you can climb down the steps using the skills in this book. Next, you'll build simple Hassle Plans for typical conflicts in your life. With practice, these Hassle Plans will become a mental program that starts quickly and automatically without you having to think about it. That way, if someone puts you down or accuses you of something, you'll automatically do the right thing. First, you'll develop plans to cope with peer hassles. These are the things your friends or other kids do that make you angry. Next, you'll develop plans to cope with adult hassles. These hassles are a bit more complicated because whether you like it or not, you don't hold all the cards when dealing with teachers, parents, and other adults. You can learn to handle these difficult situations in a way that keeps you out of trouble. Last, you'll practice these plans to make them automatic.

The Conflict Staircase

It's impossible to avoid conflict. That's a fact. Sometimes you say the wrong thing or you're not paying attention and you're in a conflict before you know it. Conflict is a bit like a staircase. You can climb up the steps toward more conflict and anger, or you can climb down the steps to de-escalate or defuse conflict and avoid trouble. A kid gives you a look and you glare at him. You just took a step up the conflict staircase. Your sister teases you and you tease her back. You just took a step up the conflict staircase. A teacher tells you to stop doing something and you insist you weren't doing it. You just took a step up the conflict staircase. With each step up, the conflict and anger build until the zero-to-60 anger kicks in and you're in trouble again.

You don't have to climb the conflict staircase. You can take one step down and then another to de-escalate the conflict and cool your anger. In this book, you've learned the tools to do this. For example, you might use your assertiveness tool to step down the conflict staircase, or you might negotiate a compromise so you and the other person both win. That's a step down the staircase. You have the tools. All it takes is for you to decide to climb down rather than up.

Handle Peer Hassles

Teasing, name calling, jokes that aren't really jokes, and rude actions are the types of hassles most teens experience with their peers. Some common ones are:

- Teasing or calling you names.
- Spreading rumors.
- Interrupting you.
- Doing an annoying habit (humming, talking while you're trying to listen to the teacher, etc.).

You can learn to handle verbal hassles like these before the anger gets out of control. The first step is to match the strategy to the hassle. Often, people with zero-to-60 anger respond to verbal hassles in just one way: anger followed by angry actions like yelling or pushing. There are other strategies to handle verbal

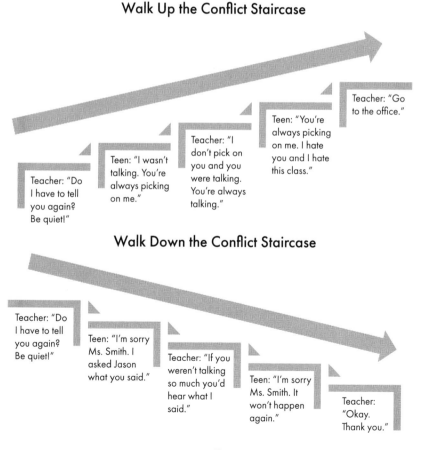

Walk Up the Conflict Staircase

Teacher: "Do I have to tell you again? Be quiet!"

Teen: "I wasn't talking. You're always picking on me."

Teacher: "I don't pick on you and you were talking. You're always talking."

Teen: "You're always picking on me. I hate you and I hate this class."

Teacher: "Go to the office."

Walk Down the Conflict Staircase

Teacher: "Do I have to tell you again? Be quiet!"

Teen: "I'm sorry Ms. Smith. I asked Jason what you said."

Teacher: "If you weren't talking so much you'd hear what I said."

Teen: "I'm sorry Ms. Smith. It won't happen again."

Teacher: "Okay. Thank you."

DEFUSING CONFLICT DO'S AND DON'TS

DO	*DON'T*
Express yourself calmly, with I-messages, and send the right non-verbal signals (smile rather than a frown or grimace).	Don't blame the person. The person has rights and wishes too.
Use your calm mind tools. Anger can cloud your read on things. What you see as unfair might not really be unfair.	Don't assume the person did this to you intentionally. Mistakes happen.
Describe the problem clearly and objectively to avoid disagreements about what is or isn't the problem. For example, "I've loaned things to you before and you gave them back to me ripped or dirty," rather than "You don't care about my stuff."	Don't try to be right. The longest and loudest arguments often occur when you try to convince the other person that you're right and that they're wrong. Try to be effective and let go of trying to be right.
Accept that it's okay to agree to disagree. In fact, that is sometimes the only way to agree about some things.	Don't react or respond to every slight or criticism. Try fogging the person's message a little, just to take the sting out of it.
Try a half-smile if you can't muster a full one. Say something nice, even when you're a little irritated. A small compliment, such as, "Hey, that was a great catch you made in the game yesterday," is a great way to de-escalate a situation. Most people feel good when someone compliments them, and feel angry when someone tears them down.	Don't clench your fists, lean toward the person, or make sarcastic remarks. This only fuels anger and escalates the conflict.

hassles that are much less likely to get you into to trouble. Four ways that usually work the best are:

- Ignore.
- Walk away.
- Assert yourself.
- Seek help.

Alejandro listed several typical situations with friends and others that upset him. He then thought through the best ways to handle the situations (ignore, walk, assert, help). Now you try it. First, look at the ABCs of Anger forms you've completed. In the Antecedent section, you'll see the typical situations with peers that tend to tick you off. On a sheet of paper, make a list of peer hassles. Think back over the last few weeks and add any conflicts with friends, siblings, or other kids to the list. Try to write a list including all the typical conflicts with peers that make you angry.

ALEJANDRO'S RESPONSES TO VERBAL PROVOCATIONS

Situation

I'm really tall for my age and I often trip or bump into something when I'm not paying attention. Some of my friends call me clumsy or "Hey, grace," to tease me.	**(Ignore)** Walk	Assert	Help
There're a couple of kids that don't know when to stop. They call me other names and keep at it.	Ignore Walk	**(Assert)**	Help
One of the kids who teases me got in my face once when I told him to knock it off. I think he's got it out for me.	Ignore **(Walk)**	Assert	Help
A kid threatens me, "Shut up or I'll hit you."	Ignore Walk	Assert	**(Help)**

Ignore

When another kid calls you a name, teases you, or provokes you, it's best not to rise to the bait. You don't necessarily step down the conflict staircase when you ignore hassles, but you don't step up the staircase either. Ignoring hassles is easier than it sounds. The anger management tools you've learned will help you keep your cool. Use deep calming breaths or calming thoughts, such as "He's not worth the time." What really helps is to have a Hassle Plan for verbal provocations. You'll learn to build Hassle Plans later in this chapter.

Walk Away

Walking away is the best response when you already know a kid or situation is certain to make you angry. Heading in the other direction when you see that kid is perhaps the best prevention strategy there is. At the same time, walking away can be difficult when you're starting to feel angry. You may want to get in the last word to save face or show the other kid that the taunts and teasing don't affect you. There are other ways to save face that will not only help you walk away but will help you avoid getting in trouble.

SAVE FACE AND WALK AWAY	
STEP 1	Pay attention to your anger level. It's best to walk away when your anger is just starting to warm up (less than 50 degrees on the "anger thermometer" you made earlier). If you wait until the anger level is higher it's much more difficult to walk away.
STEP 2	Walk away with your head held high. Don't look back. Your face might signal anger and if it does, the kid might continue to provoke you because they see that they're getting under your skin.

STEP 3 It's best not to say anything but if you have to, just say you have to go.

STEP 4 If the other kid says something to you as you walk away, just ignore it. Anything you say will only take you up the anger staircase.

STEP 5 Use the Stop the Drum Beat of Anger tools. They'll help you move on.

Assert Yourself

Assertiveness is a good response to most hassles because it defends your rights while decreasing the chance you'll climb the conflict staircase. In Chapter 6, you learned to DEAL. Use this to stand up for yourself. Don't forget the other assertiveness tools, like the Stand-Up Sandwich and the Hit the Repeat Button. You might use all these tools with one kid while with another kid DEAL will do the trick. You'll build Hassle Plans later in this chapter that include assertiveness tools. Be sure to send the right signals with your body when you DEAL. You want to send a cool, calm, and firm signal with your words, voice, and body. It helps to practice this in front of a mirror. Match your words, "Give me back my phone," with a calm body and voice.

Seek Help

Sometimes, teasing is more than teasing. Some kids will ridicule and intimidate you over and over. They're just looking for a fight and to bully you and other kids. You likely know who they are. The best way to respond to peers who are truly out to get you is to ask for help from a teacher or another adult. Asking for help is another way to assert your rights, although indirectly. It's important that teachers at your school know about bullying so they can help you.

> This morning as we walked to our next class, Benny started to tease me. Usually, I blow up and then Benny tells me I can't take a joke. That just makes me want to punch him. I decided that this time, I'd ignore Benny, and practiced some of my stay cool tools. First, I STOPPED and took a couple of slow deep breaths while I thought through what would happen if I did punch him or made a big scene. I'm already on thin ice with the principal and my parents. One more blowup will get me grounded at home or suspended from school. Then I would lose my spot on the soccer team and wouldn't be able to finish the season. No good. Next, I tried the Move to Another Seat thinking tool. I reminded myself that Benny is pretty insecure, and he teases me when he's not feeling great about himself. That helped some, too. Last, I decided that I would play through the teasing, just like I play through a side stitch in a game. It's not easy to ignore a put down. I don't like people teasing me, but I felt good about being able to cool my anger.
>
> —Alejandro

Make a Peer Hassle Plan

When people hassle you it's always the same hassles: teasing, name calling, spreading rumors, or annoying habits. These are upsetting, but if you have zero-to-60 anger, they can accelerate your anger in an instant. Peer Hassle Plans include tools to handle peer provocations as well as to prevent them in the future. You'll use ICCAN to brainstorm at least three possible choices or solutions to these typical peer hassles. These will be the solutions you'll include in the Hassle Plan. You'll also include a strategy in the Hassle Plan to prevent the hassle in the future. This is particularly helpful for hassles that tend to come up repeatedly. Look at Jason's Peer Hassle Plan on the next page. A kid in his class repeatedly kicked his chair, which made him angry. The kid didn't do it intentionally. Jason knew that it was just one of the kid's annoying habits. Still, Jason didn't want to get in trouble anymore because he lost his cool.

Handle Adult Hassles

Now that you've learned to handle hassles with peers, it's time to tackle the hassles and conflicts that can arise with your parents and teachers. These are trickier situations because—whether you like it or not—they're adults and you're not. You can learn to handle these hassles, too. Accusations—false and true—are the most common hassles that arise for teens when dealing with adults. At times, an adult will accuse you of something you didn't do. Adults make mistakes, too, and sometimes they assume you've done something when you haven't. When this happens, you'll want to set the record straight and defend your rights. It's important you do this in a way that doesn't get you into more trouble. At other times, an adult will accuse you of

JASON'S PEER HASSLE PLAN

Instructions: Describe the hassle and circle the category of the hassle. Then, use DEAL (the problem solving tool) and brainstorm at least three solutions for this problem. Rank them in the order you'll try them, where 1 means you'll try this solution first. *Remember, the best solution is the one that's most likely to work and the least likely to create more problems for you.* If the first solution doesn't work, you'll try the second solution. Last, come up with a strategy to prevent this hassle from happening again.

Describe Hassle: I'm in class and the kid sitting behind me is kicking the back of my chair. I'm having trouble concentrating and I missed a couple of things Ms. Barth said about our homework assignment.

Categories of Hassles

Interrupting You   Teasing You

Calling You Names   Damaging Your
                                           Property

Spreading Rumors about You   (Annoying Habits)

Brainstorm Three Solutions

1: Move my desk so that he can't kick it.   2: Tell him to stop.   3: Ask Ms. Barth if I can move to another seat.

Strategy I'll Use: Ask Ms. Barth if I can move my desk.

Back-Up Strategy I'll Use: Tell him to stop: "Stop kicking my desk, now."

Preventive Strategy: Ask Ms. Barth if she would move me permanently to a new seat and away from the kid who can't sit still.

something you did do. No one's perfect, and there will be times when a teacher or parent will catch you with your hand in the cookie jar. You can learn to handle both situations using the anger management tools you've learned.

False-Accusation Hassles

One of the most common anger-provoking situations is when you're accused, criticized, or blamed for something you didn't do. A teacher might accuse you of cheating on a test or copying your friend's homework when you didn't do it. Or your mom might accuse you of breaking the TV remote when your sister did it. At times, an adult might accuse you of something that you did do but for the wrong reasons. For example, a teacher might accuse you of picking on a kid when you were really defending yourself. Or your dad might accuse you of slamming the door intentionally when it was an accident. People make mistakes. They jump to the wrong conclusions sometimes. Either way, it's super important you know how to explain what happened without getting too angry. If you blow up, then you can't explain your side of things because parents, teachers, and even friends stop listening to you. When a teacher or one of your parents accuses you of something you didn't do, the first thing you might do, perhaps automatically, is defend yourself: "I didn't do it." With teachers, parents, and other adults, that tends to make things worse. They think you're disagreeing with them, and technically you are, but it makes them want to prove you wrong. As you defend yourself, they try to prove they're right, and you and the adult climb the conflict staircase—one step at a time—until you (and not the adult) are in trouble.

Good listening tools will help you climb down the conflict staircase. Rather than saying you didn't do it, try saying instead,

"What do you mean?" or "Why do you think that?" This gives the adult time to explain their version of events and enables you to figure out how they jumped to that conclusion. Once the adult clarifies the problem, you'll have a better chance to give the facts. Of course, this assumes the adult is open to hearing the facts. If you become defensive, or start yelling and screaming, the adult may no longer be open to hearing your side. In Chapter 6, you've learned to listen actively:

- *Listen* carefully to what the person is saying.
- *Repeat* what you've heard back to the person.
- *Clarify* the point or problem the person is making.

Don't forget to use calm words in a calm body, as well as I-messages. These clear communication tools will help you resolve conflicts quickly with parents, teachers, and other adults. Look at the way Ayanna used her active listening tools to handle conflict with her mom on the next page.

True Accusation Hassles

All of us sometimes are caught with our hand in the cookie jar. We do something that upsets someone, and the person is angry with us. Sometimes it's a mistake, and sometimes it's intentional, but either way, getting angry back doesn't solve the problem. Getting angry back only starts the quick climb up the conflict staircase. With each step, anger makes it more difficult for you to tell your side of the story.

Begin with a sincere apology. One of the hardest things in the world is admitting when you're wrong, but nothing defuses a conflict faster than a sincere apology. An apology calms the

AYANNA HANDLES A FALSE ACCUSATION

Ayanna's Mom	Ayanna	Tool
You haven't finished your homework. You're not going out until it's done.	You don't want me to leave until I've finished my homework.	Listen and Repeat
Yes. You know homework before fun with friends.	You think I haven't finished my homework?	Clarify
You haven't and you're not going out until you do.	I finished most of my work in study hall today so I didn't have much work to finish. I did it all. Would you like me to show you?	Provide Explanation
I'm sorry. Yes, please show me your work and then you can go.	Okay, Mom. I know you want me to do well in school.	End on the Positive

other person and signals that you're ready to fix the problem and learn from it. If you can't apologize sincerely, it's unlikely you'll be able to tell your side of the story. If you've put the other person on the defensive it's unlikely they'll listen to your side. A sincere apology opens that door. There are several ingredients that go into a sincere apology:

- A clear statement that you were wrong.
- A clear statement that you're sorry for the effect your actions had on the other person.
- A clear statement that you don't want it to happen again.

EXAMPLES OF SINCERE APOLOGIES

Situation	Apology
Alejandro's dad told him that he could play soccer with friends after he completed his homework. Instead, Alejandro left before completed all his homework.	I'm sorry, Dad. You told me that I couldn't hang out with my friends until I finished my homework, but I went out anyway. I understand that you're upset. I don't want to let you down like this again.
Ayanna's mom told her to change her shirt before she left the house. Instead, Ayanna left wearing the shirt her mom asked her to change.	I'm sorry, mom. You told me to change my shirt but I didn't. I know you're upset about me ignoring you. It was wrong of me to ignore you. I understand why you're angry with me. I won't ignore what you tell me again.
Jason's teacher asked him to stay after class so that he could speak to him about his math grade. Instead, Jason left class while his teacher waited for him.	I'm sorry, Mr. Smith. You asked me to stay after class to talk to you about my math grade. I know it was wrong to walk out and I understand that you're upset with me. I promise I'll talk to you after class tomorrow.
Camila's mom asked her not to borrow her clothes. Instead, Camila borrowed one of her mom's sweaters for photo day at school.	I'm sorry, Mom. You told me not to borrow your clothes without asking you first but I did it anyway. That was wrong of me and I understand that you're angry about this. I promise not to borrow your things again without asking you first.

Here are some examples of sincere apologies following mistakes:

Tell your side of the story. Telling your side of the story means telling the truth but in a way that shows you and your actions in the best light. When you're accused of something you did, it doesn't help to yell and scream. Anger is not the best way to explain your side of the story, especially when you did something wrong. Not only does anger cause you to act before you think, anger makes it difficult for you to explain what happened clearly.

Anger only complicates a situation that's already complicated. When you've done something wrong—either by mistake or on purpose—a parent, teacher, or another adult will decide who is right, who is wrong, and what happens next. The way you explain your side of the story can affect the decision. Try for stories with the following ingredients:

- *Tell the truth*. Telling your side of the story doesn't mean you lie or even minimize your part in the problem. It means you present the truth in a way that reflects your best self.
- *Say you're sorry*. Remember, an apology calms the other person. Also, if you did something wrong, a sincere apology can repair the relationship.
- *Don't talk too much*. If you stray too far from the facts, people get confused and frustrated, or might think you're not telling the truth. Stick to the facts and describe what happened briefly and calmly.
- *Don't blame the other person.* Nothing complicates your side of the story more than you blaming the other person for what happened. If you made a mistake, admit it.
- *Listen actively*. If you're not communicating clearly, the other person may think you're defensive or arguing. Remember to clarify and repeat to signal that you're listening to what the other person is saying.
- *Use I-statements to describe your point of view*. As you've learned, You-statements put people on the defensive. Use I-statements to explain your take on things, including how you felt. Rather than, "You never let me go out with my friends," try, "I feel upset when I can't go out with my friends because I think you don't want me to be happy."

> I'm not going to lie, I got so busted! Yesterday morning, I borrowed my Mom's new sweater without asking her first. Turns out she had a big meeting with important clients and she planned to wear it. So when she got home from work and saw me wearing it... BOOM. She was pissed. I immediately knew there wasn't any point in lying. She was mad, and started yelling all these questions at me! I could feel my anger building. So I started with an apology. It was hard, because I was already feeling defensive and angry, but it helped. She stopped, then waited for me to explain, and I did. I didn't lie, but I told the truth in a way that put me in the best light. I said, "Mom, I'm sorry. I didn't ask you if I could borrow your new sweater because I thought you would say no. That doesn't make what I did okay, I know. Your new sweater is beautiful, and I wanted to look good today. Again, I'm sorry, and I promise I'll never borrow your things without asking you first again. I hope you'll forgive me." I couldn't believe that it worked, but it did. Not only did I keep my cool, but she told me that she has days that she doesn't feel great about the way she looks, too. Even though she reminded me to not borrow her things again without asking, I felt a little closer to her.
>
> —Camilla

Vaccinate Yourself Against Hassles

Anger takes a toll on all kinds of relationships. Friends tire of dealing with your anger and walk away when they see you getting angry. Siblings start to avoid you and worry they'll say something to set off zero-to-60 anger again. Teachers and coaches start to see you as trouble and may no longer want to help you succeed at school or in sports. Parents start to worry about you and may limit their time around you, even when you're feeling cool and calm. As you practice the tools in this book and the anger fades, your relationships will improve. Once again, friends, family members, teachers, and coaches will see your strengths and possibilities. But no one is perfect. No matter how hard you've worked to cool your anger, it can still pop up: an angry word, a scowl, a sarcastic remark.

To protect yourself from these inevitable slips, try complimenting people. Harsh and angry words are like scissors. They can cut and hurt your relationships with people. Compliments—if they're kind and sincere—are like padding and can protect your relationships if you accidentally say or do something hurtful. The person is a bit less likely to hold the angry word against you because they've heard many more compliments than harsh words. Compliments over time make it easier for people to let it go and move on. Here are a few tips to follow when complimenting other people:

- *Don't overdo a compliment.* Rather than saying, "You're the best basketball player on the team," try, "Nice shot" or "good idea." Over-the-top compliments can sound insincere to people, or even sarcastic. Keep the compliments short and simple.
- *Match your body with your words.* Smile and look at people when you compliment them. If you frown or

look away, people might think you're being sarcastic. When you match your body and words, you send the signal that you're sincere, and you mean to build the relationship rather than tear it down.

- *Find the right time.* Timing is important when using compliments to rebuild and protect relationships. Don't compliment a friend after a big blowup or disagreement. People might think you don't care that you did or said something to upset or hurt the person. Apologize instead and then wait and watch for a time when things are easy and back to normal.

Build Hassle Plans

Zero-to-60 anger hits fast and hard. Anger can hit you so fast that it clouds your thinking. Anger makes it hard to think about anything else except what's in front of you. Then you act before you think and you're in trouble again. That's why it's important to build automatic mental programs to help you think on your feet and step down the conflict staircase. That's where Hassle Plans come in. Building and practicing Hassle Plans is a way to plan for the common hassles that come up in your life so you know what to do and can do it quickly. Hassle Plans include the typical situations that provoke anger. Different teens have different hassle plans because every teen is a little different.

This may sound a little complicated, but it's not. Most people just have a few situations that tend to make them angry and a few favorite tools to solve problems and resolve conflicts. The first step in building a Hassle Plan is the planning phase. You'll want to identify the typical hassles that tend to make you angry. By now, you likely know these hassles. You can look at the ABCs of Anger forms you've completed too for some ideas. Jason's typical hassles include when someone asks him to do something, when his older sister rolls her eyes at him, and when his dad asks him about school and homework. Next, you'll want to list your anger signals. Remember, these are the signals your angry body and angry mind send. The final step is to identify the tools you'll use to stay cool and climb down the conflict staircase. Hassle Plans include the tools you've learned:

- Cool body tools.
- Cool thoughts tools.
- Stop the drumbeat of anger tools.
- Communicate clearly tools.
- Solve problems tools.

After you've identified typical hassles and tools, the next thing to do is to build a Hassle Plan for each. Look at Jason's Hassle Planning form for some examples.

Practice Hassle Plans

The final step is to practice the Hassle Plans for the situations that trigger zero-to-60 anger. It's important to practice Hassle Plans if you want to build a mental program or habit that shifts into gear quickly and automatically. That way, when an event triggers your anger, you can use the skills you've learned quickly to manage the situation before it gets out of control and you get into trouble. There are six steps to practicing your Hassle Plans:

1. Build a Hassle Plan ladder. Take a look at all the Hassle Plans and rank them according to how often the hassle arises in your life (Very Likely, Likely, Least Likely). Begin with the Very Likely hassles.

JASON'S HASSLE PLANNING FORM

What typical hassles tend to frustrate you or create conflict?	What typically happens?	What would you like to happen?	What tools will you use to keep cool?
When dad talks to me about grades and homework.	I blow up, yell at him, and he grounds me.	Me and my dad work out a plan so that I can still have fun with friends and satisfy my dad too.	Slow deep breathing. STOP. Active listening. ICANN. Negotiation.
When mom tells me to clean my room.	I ignore her and then she tells dad to talk to me. Usually, I lose my cool with him.	Me and my mom decide ahead of time on a good time to clean my room that's okay with her and me, so she doesn't have to nag me later.	Slow deep breathing. STOP. Active listening. ICANN. Negotiation.
When Calvin is late.	I yell at him and he gets angry and we don't have a good time.	I ask Calvin to try to be on time, but I try to understand that he still might be late because of things out of his control. I stay cool and we have a good time even though he's late.	Slow deep breathing. STOP. ICANN. Assertiveness.
When my sister rolls her eyes at me.	I yell at her or say something sarcastic. I get in trouble and she doesn't.	Keep cool and ignore her.	Slow deep breathing. STOP. Ignore. Time machine. Assertiveness.
When my math teacher talks to me about my grades.	I blame him for my grades and get angry and walk away. He then tells my parents and they ground me.	Remind myself that he's trying to help me and listen to his suggestions.	Slow deep breathing. STOP. Active listening. Apologize. ICANN.

2. Take one of the hassles and read through the Hassle Plan. Read through it several times to remind yourself of the plan and to refresh your memory.

3. Now, go to a quiet place where no one will interrupt you. Don't practice if you're already feeling angry or just after a hassle. It's better to do this when you're feeling calm.

4. Now, close your eyes and imagine the hassle. Think about who is there, what's going on, how you're feeling in your body, and what you're thinking. Permit yourself to feel the anger. Rate the intensity of the anger (0 to 100) using the Anger Thermometer you created.

5. On your phone or another device, read your Hassle Plan aloud to record it. You'll listen to the Hassle Plan recording when you do the next step. If you can't record it, place the written Hassle Plan nearby so you can open your eyes and read it. You might look at it a couple of times as you practice.

6. As you imagine the hassle and feel angry, go through your Hassle Plan one step at a time. If you forget the steps of the plan, open your eyes and read it again. Then, close your eyes and go back to the hassle you're imagining. Keep practicing in this way until you notice you feel a little less angry when you imagine the hassle. Do this for each of the hassles and practice in this way a little every day. It will probably seem silly when you first try it, but practice like this will build your confidence that you can use the Hassle Plan quickly when a hassle actually comes up in your life.

> My Hassle Plans are helping. I'm more aware of the situations that tend to rev the anger engine, and I now know what to do to cool down. It felt a little weird to imagine my typical anger situations and then practice using my Hassle Plans, but now I'm actually starting to use my Hassle Plans almost automatically. I'm not as worried about blowing up over every little disagreement and conflict with my friends or my sister and parents because I know what to do, and it's working.
> —Jason

IN A NUTSHELL

Conflict is conflict. Whether it's conflict with a friend, another kid, or with your parents or teachers, you can't always avoid it. You can learn to step down rather than up the conflict staircase. As you've learned in this book, zero-to-60 anger causes you to act before you think. That's why so many teens with zero-to-60 anger end up in fights or screaming matches. Even though you know the right thing to say and do, anger can make it difficult for you to remember to do it. In an instant, you're in trouble again.

1. You've developed Hassle Plans to handle name-calling, teasing, and other hassles from your peers. As you use these Hassle Plans, your relationships with friends and other kids will improve. Don't forget to compliment

friends, and even your brothers, sisters, and parents. Compliments protect your relationships from anger that slips through.

2. You've developed Hassle Plans to handle adults who falsely accuse you of something you didn't do or when they accuse you rightly of something you did do. Don't forget to begin with a sincere apology to get adults to listen to you. Then, tell your side of the story. Remember, you're not lying and telling a story that isn't true. You're just telling the best version of the true story.

3. Once you've put together a set of Hassle Plans, don't forget to practice them. Remember, you're building a mental program that helps you automatically cool your anger, handle hassles, and climb down the conflict staircase.

CHAPTER 9

Build Self-Esteem and Self-Confidence

Healthy *self-esteem* means you fundamentally like yourself, even when you make a mistake, when you do something you regret, or when you lose your cool. Teens with healthy self-esteem accept and celebrate their strengths and their weaknesses. They believe they're equal to others even when they're quite different from friends and other people. When your self-esteem is weak, you're easily hurt, and when you're hurt, you can get angry. Even a little light-hearted teasing from a good friend can make you angry because it's hard for your self-esteem to take even a small hit.

Healthy *self-confidence* means you believe in yourself. You don't doubt that you have the smarts, skills, and talent to go after what you want and handle what life throws at you along the way. Healthy self-confidence is believing you have the skills and knowledge to succeed and healthy self-esteem is celebrating those successes as well as yourself. When your self-confidence is low, you might feel anxious about trying new things or performing well, and when you're anxious, you might get angry. A teacher asks you to present a report to the class. You panic and throw a book across the classroom. A coach speaks to you about the pass you missed at practice. You freak out and yell at him. These are all signs of low self-confidence.

In this chapter, you'll learn the relationship between low self-esteem and low self-confidence and how this cycle can fuel your anger. You'll learn the typical reasons people with zero-to-60 anger have low self-esteem and the importance of increasing self-esteem in order to cool anger. You'll then learn tools to boost your self-esteem and self-confidence. As you learn and practice these tools, you'll notice your self-confidence and self-esteem strengthen. You'll feel less anxious, less guilty, less angry, and more in charge of your life. Most importantly, you'll like yourself more. Not just the person your friends and family know and like, but the deep-down person that is the real you.

Self-Esteem and Self-Doubt

Although people can be very confident in one area of their lives, such as sports, and less confident in another area, such as making friends, those who are self-confident in general are more likely to succeed in life and feel happier and more comfortable in their own skins. Therefore, strengthening self-confidence strengthens self-esteem, and vice versa. Healthy self-confidence and healthy self-esteem are both necessary to succeed in life and to feel good about yourself.

Building strong self-esteem helps you feel more confident in your abilities in all areas of your life, whether it's as a student, a friend, or an athlete. Self-confident people are more willing to try new things, which means they're more comfortable taking a chance they might fail. They're more likely to persist in the face of life's bumps, too. Whereas self-confidence can vary from situation to situation, self-esteem is an everlasting part of a person's self-image. People can pick up the signs of self-doubt that accompany low self-esteem. People who slouch, look down, frequently seek reassurance, or wonder aloud whether they have what it takes to succeed, signal to others that they lack confidence.

Signs of Low Self-Esteem

Many people with low self-esteem believe they're not good enough. They might think they're not attractive, not smart, or not talented. Then there are the people who have overly high self-esteem. They're full of themselves and think they're better than everyone. A healthy self-esteem is in the middle of this range. People with healthy self-esteem accept their strengths and weaknesses and are comfortable trying and sometimes failing. The signs of low self-esteem vary from person to person, but here are the most common ones:

Over-focusing on Accomplishment

People with low self-esteem sometimes rely solely on accomplishments to boost their self-esteem. They need to succeed at all things all the time to feel good about themselves. They have a long list of accomplishments, certificates, good grades, and prizes, but accomplishments don't make them like themselves much. Because they depend only on what they accomplish in the world to feel good about themselves, that good feeling quickly passes. This is a vicious, draining cycle and people caught up in this race are stressed and unhappy. They keep adding to the list of accomplishments and the list changes as they age: a great-paying job, a great car, a big house.

This sign of low self-esteem isn't easy to spot. Parents and teachers confuse the drive to succeed with the terror of failing, but deep down, those affected know the difference.

Chronically Doubting Yourself

People with low self-esteem doubt themselves at every turn. They worry that they're not attractive enough or smart enough. They automatically doubt that they have the required skills and knowledge to succeed in the classroom, on the playing field, or when hanging out with friends. People who doubt themselves believe they will fail before they even try, so often they just don't try.

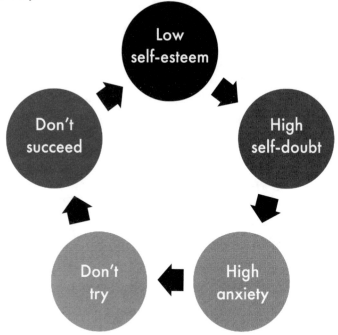

Overly Sensitive to Criticism

This is the ouch-anger arc. People with low self-esteem are easily hurt. They tend to wear their feelings on their sleeve. They often take the innocent remarks of friends, parents, and teachers personally. People may have told them that they're too sensitive, but that hurts too. It's hard for people with low self-esteem to take feedback from friends, teachers, and parents, but taking feedback and making changes based on that feedback is how we become more successful versions of ourselves.

Difficulty Accepting Compliments

People with low self-esteem have trouble taking in the nice things people say to them. They often look down and say, "Anyone could have made that pass," or, "It was an easy exam," or, "I got lucky." It's difficult for them to accept compliments because deep down they don't believe them.

Difficulty Asking for Something

People with low self-esteem can have difficulty asking for what they want. If they're having trouble understanding a math problem, they might not ask a friend or their teacher for help. They might not ask a friend to go to a movie or to come over to hang out. They have difficulty asking for what they want because they think they don't deserve someone's time, attention, or caring.

Difficulty Saying No

People with low self-esteem often have difficulty saying no to the requests of others. This means that other people often take advantage of them. Other kids might ask to copy their homework, or for them to steal something for them from a store. People with low self-esteem might do these things because if you have a low opinion of yourself you might do anything to gain the positive opinion and attention of others.

Feeling Ashamed After a Failure

Shame is one of the main signs of low self-esteem. Shame is a powerful feeling and is not the same as guilt. You feel guilty when you do something wrong or bad, such as lying to a friend. You feel shame when you do something and believe this means that you are bad, as in "I'm a bad, horrible, disgusting person," because you lied to a friend. People with low self-esteem feel deeply ashamed for the small mistakes and failures that everyone makes.

Trying to Be Perfect

People with low self-esteem often try to prove to themselves that they're smart, talented, and attractive by trying too hard. They try to be perfect, but of course they can't. No one can. They set unrealistic goals for themselves, such as getting straight A-pluses on every test, quiz, and homework assignment. Then, when they fail to do this, they feel ashamed and, worse yet, see this as evidence that they're stupid, lame, or lazy. You name it.

Amplifying the Negative

People with low self-esteem see the world, and particularly themselves, through the shrinking end of binoculars. They shrink their accomplishment and their strengths. When they make a mistake they shrink themselves into a box: "I'm an idiot," or "I'm a loser." People with low self-esteem have a glass-half-empty attitude toward life. They focus on shortcomings and miss the rest. When they miss a shot, fail a quiz, or lose a friend, they amplify the negative rather than stepping back and seeing the bigger picture. (Examples of seeing the bigger picture could be: "I missed a shot but made most of them." "I failed a quiz but passed the big exam." "I lost a friend but I still have many other great and close ones.")

Exaggerating

People with low self-esteem tend to exaggerate their accomplishments in order to feel better about themselves. They might brag that they're the smartest kid in school or the best player on the team. For some this may be true, but for most people it's not. Exaggerating tends to backfire because people see through exaggeration and don't like it. Friends want friends who are more like them and when people exaggerate they signal that they think they're better than everyone else. This tends to push old friends and potential friends away.

Putting Others Down

People with low self-esteem often believe that the only way to feel better about themselves is to level the playing field by bringing others down. They try to pull people down from their pedestals—when your opinion of yourself is low enough, *everyone* else is on a pedestal, but of your own making. People with low self-esteem call other people names or tear down their accomplishments because they think that then they'll feel better about themselves.

Blaming Others

It's difficult for people with low self-esteem to admit that they're wrong or that they've made a mistake. When they're feeling bad about themselves, they might want to find someone to blame. If they believe that they're a victim of circumstance or of other people's actions, rather than an imperfect person who sometimes makes mistakes, then there isn't really anything wrong with them. If they miss a shot, it's because a teammate didn't pass the ball well. If they don't do well on a quiz, it's because the teacher has it in for them.

Anger and Self-Esteem

Imagine you're walking through the kitchen and hit your head on a cabinet door someone left open. Ouch! Automatically, you feel angry and you slam the cabinet door. This is the ouch-anger arc. When someone or something hurts us, we want to stop it and anger motivates us to do that. When someone kicks your leg, you get angry in order to stop the kid from kicking you again. When you bump your head on a cabinet door, your anger stops the cabinet from hitting you again. Well, probably not. Anger doesn't always make sense. The ouch-anger arc is a normal, natural, and automatic response to hurt.

The ouch-anger arc works for emotional hurt, too. When your self-esteem takes a hit, it hurts, just like when your shin takes a hit on the soccer field. When a teacher reprimands you, it hurts your pride, it hurts your feelings, it hurts your self-esteem. You go from ouch to anger in a flash. When your self-esteem is weak, the emotional ouch is intense and so is the anger that comes out of it.

When your self-esteem is healthy and strong, you can take the hits that come with the ups and downs of life. You can shrug off the hit your self-esteem takes when you do poorly on a test, when you lose a soccer game, when a friend ignores you, when a kid teases you a little, or a teacher accuses you of something that isn't true. When your self-esteem is strong enough, these hits don't hurt as much, and your anger doesn't go from zero to 60 in seconds.

When your self-esteem is weak, the smallest setback or slight threat and your danger alarm goes off. That's when anger might step forward to defend your self-esteem. If your self-esteem is low, so is your self-confidence, and this fuels your anxiety, fear, and ultimately your anger. If you're terrified you'll flunk your math exam because you doubt you're smart enough to pass, you might lash out at friends, at your tutor, or at your math teacher. Anger sends a signal to others to back off. If you feel overwhelmed by all the demands parents, teachers, and friends place on you, your anger flares and people might give you a pass.

Factors That Lower Self-Esteem

Now that you know the signs of low self-esteem, it's time to consider the factors that can lower it and keep it low. The tools later in this chapter will help you boost and strengthen your self-esteem over time. The most common factors that lower self-esteem are messages from others, messages from the world, and messages from yourself.

Messages From Others

Messages from the important people in your life—friends, parents, teachers—can shape how you see yourself. People who are kind and give you reasonable and caring feedback about your strengths and weaknesses can help you become a better version of yourself. People who always tell you that you could do better, be better, or you're not okay the way you are, weaken self-esteem and keep it weak. Like anger, low self-esteem tends to run in families. This kind of makes sense if you think about it. An aunt with low self-esteem might put you down to build herself up. A brother who doesn't like himself might criticize you to help him feel better about himself. A relative who pushes himself because he doesn't believe he's good enough might push you too much as well. Although you may not be able to stop the people in your life from sending you certain messages, you can decide which messages you want to believe and which messages you don't.

Look at the self-esteem family tree. You can copy the next page or draw your own tree to make your own self-esteem family tree with the names of your family members (fill in whoever you're closest to, or whoever you think would work best for this exercise). Then, circle a (+) if you think the family member has positive self-esteem. Circle a (-) if you think the family member has negative self-esteem. Circle a (o) if you don't know. Don't forget to write your name on the family tree. Is your self-esteem positive or negative?

+ o -   + o -   + o -   + o -
_____ _____   _____ _____

        + o -   + o -
        _____   _____

+ o -   + o -   + o -   + o -   + o -
_____ _____ _____ _____ _____
                Me

Messages From the World

If you're like most people, you're bombarded by messages from the world. You're not thin enough. You're not buff enough. You're not smart or talented enough. These days, most of the messages come from advertisements, TV shows, movies, and social media. Social media can be particularly hard on your self-esteem. Although social media helps connect you to other people, it only connects you to what those people want to show you. You don't see their real lives. People carefully select and present the most positive and interesting parts of their lives and create an ideal version of themselves. It's natural to compare yourself to others, but as you compare yourself to these ideals, you might begin to believe you're not attractive enough, not smart enough, not rich enough, or not good enough in general. These messages aren't going away and it's unlikely you'll get off social media just to stop seeing them (but hey, give it a try for 30 days and see what happens!). But just like the messages other people send you, you can decide which messages you do want to believe and which messages you don't, even those social media messages.

Messages You Send to Yourself

The truth is, you don't have much control over the messages others send. You can only decide whether you wish to believe them. You have far more control over the messages you send yourself, and how you feel about yourself today and tomorrow depends partly on these messages. Some messages you send yourself will beat down your self-esteem and increase self-doubt, while others will boost your self-esteem and decrease self-doubt. The following tools will help you learn to talk to yourself differently, treat yourself better, pay attention to what is helpful, and distance yourself from things that hurt.

Boost Your Self-Esteem

Many of the tools you've learned so far can help boost your self-esteem. You can strengthen your self-esteem by taking care of your physical health. Eating right, getting sufficient exercise, and receiving enough sleep can make a big difference in how you feel about yourself. Communicating clearly with friends, teachers, and parents can help you feel connected with good friends, and good and caring friends can remind you that you're worthwhile when you doubt it. Solving problems can boost self-esteem, too. If you're quickly and effectively solving the problems life throws your way, you're more likely to be successful. Nothing builds self-esteem like small and consistent successes. Here are a few more tools you can learn and practice that will boost your self-esteem and strengthen it over time.

Practice Accepting Yourself

Self-acceptance is, obviously, the act of accepting oneself. This includes accepting your abilities and limitations, as well as what you like and dislike about yourself. Self-acceptance is the expression of deep caring and understanding. With self-acceptance comes self-compassion, and these are the foundations of healthy self-esteem. It's far easier to accept someone you like than it is to accept someone you don't like. That's why it can be difficult for people with low self-esteem to accept themselves. For that same reason, many people with low self-esteem feel threatened by others and unsafe in the world in general. Consequently, many people with low self-esteem are angry at themselves and others. You can develop greater self-acceptance. It just takes practice.

Write a caring letter to yourself. Over the years, you may have been sending critical and mean messages to yourself. These messages point out your shortcomings and your mistakes. If these are the only messages you send to yourself, it doesn't take long to start feeling bad about yourself. You can change this, though. You can practice writing actual letters or notes to yourself that are caring, compassionate, and inspiring. It might take some time to actually believe the kind and good things about yourself, but that's okay. Keep at it. Here are the steps:

1. Identify something that makes you feel bad about yourself. It might be something that makes you feel sad, embarrassed, ashamed, or angry. Stick to the facts, and avoid your opinions and interpretations. So "school can be hard for you," not "you're dumb." Or "sometimes you have a hard time remembering and showing up for things," not "you're a bad friend." Try to be as honest as possible. Remember, only you will read what you write.

2. Next, imagine there's someone who loves and accepts you unconditionally for who you are. What would that person say to you about this part of yourself? Write this down.

3. In the letter, remind yourself that everyone has things about themselves they don't like, and no one is perfect. Think about how many other people in the world could be struggling with the same thing you are.

4. Consider the ways in which events or the family environment you grew up in may have contributed to this negative characteristic.

5. In an accepting way, ask yourself whether there are things you could do to improve or better cope with this negative characteristic. Focus on how constructive changes could

make you feel happier, healthier, or more fulfilled, and avoid judging yourself.

After you finish the letter, put it in a safe, private place. Each day read the caring letter to yourself or aloud. Read the letter before you leave for school in the morning and before you go to bed at night. Read the letter during difficult times or when you're feeling stressed, anxious, sad, or angry. Over time, as you become more caring toward yourself, you might want to write a second letter or a third and then read those, too. Check out Jason's caring letter to himself.

Dear Jason,

It's not easy being you. I know you're frustrated that school isn't easier for you. I understand that it's upsetting to work so hard and to still not do as well as you would like. I know that you want to do well in school and that you work hard. I understand why you sometimes think, "What's the point?" I'm proud of you because you continue to try. Because of your learning challenges, you work ten times harder than most kids.

You don't have to beat yourself up so much. You compare yourself to other kids who have an easier time with school work. There's no point in comparing yourself to these kids. You're completely different. You grew up with different parents and a different brain and in different circumstances. None of these things are your fault and it's not fair to compare yourself to kids who haven't had to struggle with the stuff you've struggled with.

You've endured a lot and you've come a long way. Remember how hard it was just a few years ago. Things are getting a little easier every year and you deserve all the credit for that. You've worked very hard to get where you are even though you sometimes forget this. You're only 14 years old. You have plenty of time.

I know sometimes it seems easier to beat yourself up than it is to encourage yourself, but you can be a good friend to yourself, too. You might feel like you're the only kid who has ever struggled in school, but you know that's not true. Your dad has told you many times that school was very hard for him too.

That's why he tells you that he admires you
so much. Still, every day you fight through
a lot of shame, guilt, fear, and anger. That's
probably going to go on for a while longer, but
it will get better because it already has gotten
better—at least a little.

You're a good person, Jason. You care about
your friends and they care about you. Your
mom and dad love you, even though they
sometimes say things that hurt your feelings.
I know that you'll keep trying because that's
the kind of guy you are—but even if you didn't,
you're still okay. Nothing will change that.

Sincerely,

Jason

Meditate on self-acceptance. Responding to hurt with self-acceptance is contrary to the ouch-anger arc. When you're hurt you might take it out on yourself. You might have been doing this for so long you don't think you can treat yourself any other way. But you know how to respond to hurt with acceptance. You do this with your friends who feel hurt or who are having a hard time. It's true that responding to your own hurt with acceptance is a different story—it's more difficult! But with practice, you can learn. Start by recording the self-acceptance script below and save it in your phone (or anything that can record). Pause for one or two minutes at each step. This will create a recording that's about 10 minutes long. In addition, you can listen to the caring and compassion recording you made in Chapter 5.

1. First, make yourself comfortable. Once you're settled, close your eyes or soften your gaze and tune in to your breath. Notice your breath, without trying to change it. And notice also if you feel tense or relaxed, without trying to change that either.

2. Inhale through your nose and then exhale through your mouth. Continue to take deep, full breaths in through your nose and out through your mouth. As you breathe, become aware of the state of your body and the quality of your mind. Where is your body holding tension? Do you feel closed off from your emotions? Where is your mind? Is it wandering, or is it at home within the breath? Is your mind at ease or filled with restlessness, frustration, and doubt?

3. Place both hands over your heart and continue to inhale through your nose and exhale through your mouth. Ask yourself: How does it feel to place my hands over this tender area, this place where I experience love for self and others?

4. Let your breath become smoother and more effortless. Begin to breathe in and out through your nose. Feel the flow of air moving into your lungs and then back out into the world.

5. With each exhale, imagine you are releasing any negative thoughts that may be lingering in your mind.

6. Continue to focus on your breath. On each inhale, think "I am okay," and on each exhale, "I am enough." Let each inhale draw in self-acceptance and each exhale release what is no longer helpful to you. Take a few minutes to breathe and recite "I am okay" and "I am enough" internally. Notice how you feel as you say these words to yourself.

7. If your mind wanders at any point, know that it's okay. It's the nature of the mind to wander. Simply bring your attention back to the breath. Notice how your thoughts come and go, whether positive or negative, and simply allow them to pass on by like clouds floating in the sky.

8. Now visualize yourself standing in front of a mirror, and look into your own eyes. What do you see? Hurt and anger? Hurt and sadness? Love and joy? Neutral?

9. Regardless of what appears in the reflection, tell yourself: "I love you," "You are beautiful," and "You are worthy of happiness." Know that what you see in the mirror in this moment may be different from what you see the next time you look.

10. Imagine now that you could breathe into your heart and visualize love pouring out of your hands and into your heart.

11. Let this love warm and permeate you from your heart center, filling the rest of your body.

12. Feel a sense of comfort and calm traveling up through your chest into your neck and head, out into your shoulders, arms, and hands, and then down into your ribs, belly, pelvis, legs, and feet.

13. Allow a sensation of warmth to fill you from head to toe. Breathe here and know that acceptance is always available for you when you need it.

14. When you're ready, take a few more deep, mindful breaths and then softly open your eyes. Sit for a few moments to acknowledge the unique experience you had during this meditation. This is a beautiful opportunity to learn something new about yourself and tune into your physical and emotional needs. Let self-acceptance enable you to build a stronger relationship with yourself and allow you to show up more fully in your life.

Keep a gratitude journal. When your self-esteem is low, you likely spend time dwelling on the things you don't have rather than on the things you do. You likely compare yourself to others and focus on a quality (intelligence, creativity, strength, beauty, etc.) that you think friends and other kids have but that you think you don't. Gratitude is a great salve for the things that hurt us. Just a few moments of gratitude can make you feel happier, safer, and less angry. Gratitude is a wonderful thing on which to rest your mind, particularly during difficult times.

Keeping a journal is a great way to spend time with gratitude. Writing down the things for which you feel grateful builds the connection between the things you're grateful for and your emotional self.

Three times each week, write up to five things for which you feel grateful. Don't list these things in your head. It's very important that you *write* these in a journal or on a notepad. Writing builds the connection between the things for which you're grateful and your emotional self. Your gratitude journal might include relatively big things, such as "We won the soccer championship." However, it's important to write small things for which your grateful (like "the chocolate chip cookie I had at lunch today") too. In fact, it's likely more important to write the small things, because they happen more often and are the things we tend to ignore. The goal of the exercise is to remember a good event, experience, person, or thing in your life—then enjoy the good emotions that come with it. This is what it means to spend some time with gratitude. Here's how to do it:

1. Try to be as specific as possible. The more specific your description, the more likely you'll take in the gratitude. For example, "I'm grateful that Luke shared half of his PBJ sandwich with me today," is better than "I'm grateful Luke gave me something to eat today."

2. It's better to describe something for which you are grateful in detail than to quickly list many things without much detail. For example, "I'm grateful for the strength of my legs, lungs, and heart during soccer practice," rather than, "I'm grateful I can run."

3. As much as possible, it's better to focus on people to or for whom you are grateful rather than things for which

you're grateful. The kindness, caring, and compassion people show you is far more important than a second helping of mashed potatoes at dinner.

4. List the negative outcomes you avoided, escaped, prevented, or turned into something positive. You can be grateful for these, too. This way you don't take good fortune for granted.

5. See good things that come to you as "gifts." Seeing them as gifts will encourage you to appreciate them more.

6. Record events that were unexpected or surprised you. You're likely to feel more grateful for unexpected gifts and good fortunes, because they're above and beyond what usually comes to you.

7. Write regularly. Whether you write every other day or once a week, commit to a regular time to journal, then stick to that commitment.

Meditate on gratitude. Another way to spend time with gratitude is to listen to a recording of a gratitude meditation. You can find one on a meditation app or you can record the following script and listen to that. Gratitude isn't just about being thankful for the good things in your life, it's about being thankful for everything in your life. Part of gratitude is recognizing your good fortune and appreciating the little things that can make a big difference. If you want to make your own gratitude meditation, record this gratitude meditation script on your phone or other device. Try to make a recording that's about 10 minutes long.

1. To begin, find a safe, quiet place where no one is likely to disturb you. Sit or lie down on your back in a comfortable place. Make sure you'll be warm enough. Loosen any restrictive clothing so that you can breathe comfortably.

2. Close your eyes and take a slow, deep breath to bring yourself into the present moment and begin the process of feeling more peaceful and centered. Breathe into the belly so it expands as you breathe in and gets smaller as you breathe out.

3. Now, take a minute or two to mentally scan your body for any areas where there is tightness, tension, or soreness, and breathe your warm, oxygen-filled breath into that area. As you breathe out, release the tension. [5 second pause]

4. Now, notice any worries, fear, anger, irritation, jealousy, or judgment. Just breathe into those emotions, noting them, and allowing them to flow out as you breathe out. [5 second pause]

5. Now that your body and mind are calm and clear, focus on the events, experiences, people, pets, or possessions for which you feel grateful. [5 second pause] Recall these special gifts:

   - The gift of life itself, the most precious gift. Someone gave birth to you, someone fed you as an infant, changed your diaper, clothed you, bathed you, taught you to speak and to understand.
   - The gift of your senses, connecting you to the world— whether it's the song of a bird, the the feel of the wind or the soft grass, the taste of a favorite treat, the smell of fresh-baked bread, or the view of a beautiful sunset.

- The gift of a heartbeat, steady, regular, moment after moment, pumping fresh, life-giving blood to all your organs. [5 second pause]

6. Now think about all the things we have today that make our lives easier and more comfortable than they were for our great-grandparents:

   - We flip a switch, and light appears.
   - We turn a tap and clean, drinkable water flows.
   - We adjust a thermostat, and a room grows warmer or cooler.
   - We have a roof to keep us dry when it rains, walls to keep out the cold wind, windows to let in the light, screens to keep out insects.
   - We enter a vehicle and it takes us where we want to go.
   - We have access to machines that wash our clothes. And we have clothes to wear, and places to store them.
   - There are machines that store our food at just the right temperature and help us cook it.
   - We have indoor plumbing.
   - We have public libraries with thousands of books, free for anyone to borrow and read.
   - We have public schools that can teach us to read and write, skills that were available to only the very few just a few hundred years ago. [5 second pause]

7. Now, take a moment to reflect on all the thousands of people who have worked hard, some without knowing you at all, to make your life easier or more pleasant.

- People who plant, grow, and harvest your food.
- People who transport that food to market.
- A team of people who make the roads and railways to make it easier to transport the food.
- Another team who maintain those vehicles. And drivers, loaders, unloaders.
- Those who take the time to design the store, the shelves, the packaging that keeps the food safe and allows you to find what you need.
- Postal workers who sort and deliver the mail.
- Those who maintain the servers so you can access the Internet.
- Those who design operations and systems for gathering, sorting, and disposing of trash and recycling.
- Those who gather news stories and photos to keep you informed and amused.
- Those who play sports, create art or music, or write plays, poems, or films that entertain you.

   And most of these are people you have never met or barely know.

8. Now, consider the people and pets you know who enrich your life: those who smile at you and cheer you on; those family, friends, acquaintances, colleagues, and peers; those ancestors who worked so you could live well; those friends who support you when you need a shoulder to cry on or a helping hand. [5 second pause]

9. Now, take a moment to reflect on your own reasons for feeling grateful in this moment. [15 second pause]

10. There is so much to feel grateful for in this moment now. [10 second pause] Gratitude fills our hearts and minds, uplifting our spirit. [10 second pause]

11. When you finish, rest quietly for several minutes, noticing how you feel throughout your body, emotions, and thoughts compared with before you started. Not judging, just noticing. Gently stretch your hands and arms, feet and legs. If you choose to stand, do so slowly.

Practice Liking Yourself

People with low self-esteem don't like themselves all that much. They wouldn't take themselves to the prom. They wouldn't vote for themselves for school president. But you can learn to like yourself in the same way you can learn to like skateboarding, or painting in watercolors, or baking bread. It takes practice and an openness to the possibility that you're worth liking on the surface and deep down.

Write a letter of recommendation for yourself. One day, students or former employees who are applying to schools or jobs might ask you to write letters of recommendation for them. A letter of recommendation highlights the positive strengths of the applicant while also describing in a fair and balanced way the applicant's weaknesses. A good letter of recommendation balances praise and criticism. People with low self-esteem send messages or self-talk to themselves—perhaps every day—that favor criticism over praise. When someone receives these unbalanced and overcritical messages all the time, they start to believe them! To build a healthy self-esteem, try writing actual balanced letters to yourself. Check out Alejandro's letter of recommendation to himself.

Dear Alejandro,

It's with great pleasure that I write a letter of recommendation for Alejandro. I have known Alejandro for 14 years and I have observed him in a variety of situations: at school; at home; on the soccer field; and with friends, teachers, and his family. In all these situations, Alejandro has worked hard to stay calm and do well.

Persistence is the word that I think of when I think of Alejandro. School has always been difficult for Alejandro, particularly math. But Alejandro's difficulty with math hasn't beaten him. Alejandro continues to try, although at times he puts off doing his homework. I understand why. School work is difficult and he has to work harder than most kids.

Athletic is another word that describes Alejandro. He is great at any sport and his math difficulties have never gotten in the way of him reading another player or the action on the field. He is strong, fast, and has a great mental game. Alejandro is great at sports, but he doesn't always believe it. He can doubt his skills sometimes, particularly before big games, but he is working with his coach on this and gets more confident every practice and game.

Loyalty is another word that describes Alejandro. The anger has created some problems with his friendships, but Alejandro is willing to apologize when he makes a mistake and his friends always forgive him. They know that he's working on keeping cool. He is a loyal friend and has had the same best friends since kindergarten. Even though some old friends aren't friends anymore, he still likes them and would be their friend again if they wanted to be friends again too.

In conclusion, I highly recommend Alejandro. He is persistent and a great athlete and a

good friend. Alejandro isn't perfect but he's a
great guy and if you give him a chance you
will like him and become a good friend too.
Sincerely,
Alejandro

Savor the good stuff about yourself. You learned to savor the good and pleasant in Chapter 5. You can learn to savor the good stuff about yourself, too. You can savor the time you made the final goal that won a soccer game or the B you got on the super difficult math quiz. Savoring the good stuff is another way to practice liking yourself. Not only does savoring the good stuff about yourself boost your self-esteem, it also creates pleasant feelings that combat stress, worry, and anger. Here are the steps to savor the good stuff about yourself:

1. First, list six good things about yourself (for example, you have great balance on a skateboard) or things people complimented you about (maybe you have great style!) or successes you have had (like a good grade on a pop quiz).

2. Now, for each of the good things about yourself, write these:
   - Describe where you were and what was happening.
   - Describe the good feelings you felt (happy, proud, satisfied, etc.).
   - Describe what you were thinking when you were feeling good about yourself.

- Describe your role in making this good thing happen ("I called out to Jay to remind him to pass to me a little more").

3. Now that you've written more about the good stuff about you, read through your list again. Try to imagine this as a story about an accomplishment or a time when you felt good about yourself.

4. Finally, close your eyes, replay the story in your mind, and savor the good stuff.

Try fair comparisons. Most people measure themselves against other people. Am I smarter than her? Am I more attractive than him? Am I more talented, stronger, creative, taller, you name it, than this kid or that one? Although comparing is normal and natural, comparing can push down your self-esteem if you don't make fair comparisons. If you want to feel good about yourself as a soccer player, don't compare yourself to the best soccer player in the league. It's kind of like comparing a pepperoni pizza to a Hawaiian pizza. They're both pizzas, but boy do they taste different. If you want to decide who makes the best peperoni pizza in town, don't throw in a Hawaiian pizza. Instead, try fair comparisons. Compare yourself to all the members of your team and not only the best players. Compare yourself to all the girls in your class and not only the most popular. To practice making fair comparisons, try the pizza-to-pizza exercise. Check Alejandro's pizza-to-pizza exercise to see how this worked for him.

PIZZA TO PIZZA

Instructions: Identify the quality, skill, or aspect of the person to whom you're comparing yourself. Rate how bad you feel about yourself (0 to 100, where 100 is the worst you can imagine feeling). Next, list the strengths and weakness of the person. Try to look at the entire person and don't get stuck on the one thing you're comparing yourself to. Next, rate the importance of each strength and weakness from 0 to 100, where 100 is most important quality to everyone and everywhere. Then, do the same thing for yourself. Last, rate how bad you feel about yourself after you completed the pizza-to-pizza exercise.

Comparison: He's smarter than me.

Bad feeling before (0-100): __80__

Tom Pizza

Strengths (Pepperoni)	Importance	Weaknesses (Anchovies)	Importance
He's good at spelling.	50	His ball control is bad.	90
He gets pretty good grades.	80	He slacks off some times.	80
He's good at math.	60	He's stuck up.	90

Me Pizza

Strengths (Jalapenos)	Importance	Weaknesses (Broccoli)	Importance
I'm the fastest guy on the team.	80	I'm a slow reader.	60
I draw pretty well.	75	I lose my temper sometimes.	70
I work really hard at everything.	90	I'm not a good speller.	80

Bad feeling after (0-100): __45__

IN A NUTSHELL

Self-confidence is great. Self-confidence gets the job done because you believe you can do the job. Strong self-esteem is even more important. With a strong self-esteem you believe no matter how many mistakes you've made, you're still okay.

1. Remember, strong self-esteem protects you from the hurts everyone feels from time to time. When life's setbacks don't hurt as much, you'll worry less about making mistakes, or failing to succeed in academics, in sports, and in your friendships. You'll feel more comfortable and confident, and that will encourage you to try more things and succeed more often.

2. Remember, you swim in a sea of messages. Messages friends, teachers, and parents send you. Messages the media sends you. Messages you send to yourself. Although you can't stop all the messages others send, you can decide whether to buy into them. That includes the messages you send to yourself.

3. Don't forget to practice liking and accepting yourself. The first sign of a weak self-esteem is that you don't like who you are. You're neither good nor bad. You're a complicated mix of strengths and weakness. Like your strengths and accept your weaknesses. That's the formula for building strong and healthy self-esteem.

CHAPTER 10

Nutrition, Exercise, and Sleep

As you've learned, anger is a mixture of what is going on in your mind and what is going on in your body. Scientists have known for a long time that changes in the brain can cause changes in the body, and vice versa. In order to manage your anger, it's necessary to manage the basics: nutrition, exercise, and sleep.

In this chapter, you'll learn how healthy eating, getting enough exercise, and plenty of sleep are essential to managing anger and irritation over time.

Eat Healthy

Puberty and adolescence are times during which your body grows rapidly and, therefore, requires more calories and nutrients. During the teenage years, academic and athletic demands often increase, making it even more important that you fuel your body with the proper nutrients. Unfortunately, as demands on your time, attention, and energy have increased, it can be more difficult for you to eat in a healthy way. You might skip meals, snack on sugary and processed foods, and eat on the go. When you fill your body with foods high in saturated fats, or refined sugars, or if you skip meals and eliminate key nutrients, your body can't operate optimally and can leave you vulnerable to irritability and anger.

This next section provides some basic recommendations from the World Health Organization about how to improve your eating habits to ensure your mind and body function well. You'll also learn which foods can upset and irritate your body, and cause a range of unpleasant reactions, including anger. If you're concerned about your nutritional habits, have a medical condition that requires dietary modifications, or if you believe you're over or under weight, speak to your physician or a nutritionist about your concerns.

Healthy Eating Plan

Deciding what foods to include and what foods to avoid in your daily diet is a challenging task. Television, radio, news stories, and even social media bombard us with dietary and nutritional advice, advertisements promote convenience foods, and fads about eating and dieting that come and go. At times, it can be difficult to know what to believe. And you might feel pressured to "fit-in" and give up a healthy lunch from home in favor of something from a vending machine, or go on a diet because you're worried about how you look. Having a busy schedule that keeps you away from home for most of the day doesn't help either. Therefore, the trick to maintaining healthy eating habits is to have a plan.

Develop Healthy Eating Habits

Scientists and medical professionals are increasingly concerned about eating habits and believe these habits have contributed to a dramatic increase of obesity in both adults and youth in the world. In response, the World Health Organization created general guidelines to promote health and reduce risk of illness. The guidelines recommend:

- Choose wisely from *all* food groups.
- Strike a balance between what you eat and what you do.
- Get the most nutrition from your calories.

Choose wisely from all food groups. A healthy diet includes flexible and balanced meal planning with little, if any, restrictions. To achieve this, consider the rule of thirds as a quick and easy guide. Include in each meal 1/3 protein (meat or beans), 1/3 fruits and vegetables, and 1/3 carbohydrates (grains and starch). In addition, include some oils, fats, and salt (which is often already present in many foods) in your meals, as well as key vitamins and minerals, such as vitamin A, C, D, iron, and calcium. For additional guidance with meal planning, speak with your physician or nutritionist.

Strike a balance between what you eat and what you do. Eat moderate-sized portions and get a moderate level of physical activity daily. Eating large meals when you're not physically active means you're out of balance. Similarly, when you limit what you eat and exercise excessively, you're out of balance too.

Get the most nutrition from your calories. Smart food choices will help you to get the most nutrition from what you eat. One Kit Kat bar has 218 calories. A pack of three skim-milk cheese sticks has 216 calories (72 calories each). If you're planning a snack, cheese sticks provide far nutrition than a chocolate bar, even though the calories are about the same. But in general, fruits, veggies, and a diet that emphasizes vegetables over meat and olive oil over butter and cheese, seem to be best. Dairy and gluten are two food groups that, when eliminated, often result in people feeling better.

Build a Balanced Diet

Harvard University recently developed food guidelines called the Healthy Eating Plate. The Healthy Eating Plate recommends you include four main food groups in your daily diet: (1) vegetables, (2) fruits, (3) whole grains, (4) protein foods. It also recommends using healthy oils (limiting butter and avoiding trans fat) and drinking more water, tea, and coffee than sugary drinks and dairy. Their plan uses an easy-to-remember plate image showing approximately how much of your plate should be devoted to each food group. Their website has this visual and lots of information on each food group that can help you develop a healthy-eating plan. Alternatively, speak to your parents about setting up an appointment with a nutritionist. Nutritionists are experts at helping create meal plans tailored to teens.

Read Food Labels

Reading and understanding a Nutrition Facts food label can help you select the type and quantity of healthy foods to include in your meals and snacks. Food labels provide information about the nutrients in the food and the recommended percent daily value of each nutrient based on a 2000-calorie diet (although you may require more or fewer calories in your diet). Next time you pick up a package of food, look for the Nutrition Facts food label. It's easy to find and is usually on the side or back of most food packages. The recommended serving size of the particular food is at the top of the label, as well as the number of servings in each container. The label then lists the quantity of nutrients and vitamins found in a single serving of that food in grams or milligrams (1/1000 of a gram) and percent daily nutritional value. Most foods contain fat, carbohydrates, protein, and fiber, as well as vitamins A, C, and D, and minerals, such as calcium and iron. The purpose of the label is to provide you, the consumer, with a uniform method to plan the type and quantity of the foods to include in your meal or snack to maintain a healthy diet. In particular, check the food label for the amount of calcium in the food. Most teens get too little calcium and vitamins, and the food label can help to make sure you get a sufficient amount of these in your diet each day. To learn more about how to read and use Nutrition Fact labels to plan your meals, speak with a nutritionist or google "how to read nutrition labels"—the Food and Drug Administration (FDA), The American Heart Association, and the National Institutes of Health (NIH) all have good guides.

Look for Healthy Convenience Meals

Foods you eat at home can sometimes be just as unhealthy as a fast-food double cheeseburger with all the fixings. Healthy fast food is possible! For example, substitute a baked potato for those fries, and drink milk instead of soda. Choose a single burger without all the extra sauces, or a baked fish filet. Skip the creamy dressing on your salad and try oil and vinegar instead. Finally, remember: everything in moderation. It's best to eat a little of everything rather than cutting certain foods out altogether. Depriving ourselves of certain foods can make us crave these foods and then eat too much of them when we give in to the craving. Making a lunch out of a burger, fries, and a shake, while not an ideal meal, is less harmful if you eat this lunch once a month versus once a day.

> I didn't want to cut fast food from my diet. I like chocolate shakes and fries too much to do that! So, I tried compromising when I could, like getting a kiddie portion of a shake instead of a regular size, and splitting fries with a friend rather than having my own. I also convinced my friends to eat at the farmers market by our school on Fridays instead of eating fast food, since they have some vendors with healthier "home-cooked" and locally sourced lunch options that are actually really good. I feel like I'm being healthier, but I still get to eat my favorite foods, so I don't feel like I'm missing out.
>
> —Emma

Avoid Caffeine, Sugar, and Other Irritants

Certain foods and substances can irritate your anger. While not everyone is sensitive to these foods, for some, certain foods or substances cause them to feel tense and irritable and set them up for an anger outburst.

Caffeine is a stimulant that can trigger stress, tension, and irritability mere minutes after you ingest it. Interestingly, even low doses of caffeine—like from a chocolate bar or soda—can cause you to feel irritable, agitated, or moody: all factors that can set you up for an anger outburst. In addition, if you're allergic to certain foods, you can feel angry, dizzy, irritable, confused, or moody. You may have headaches and trouble sleeping. These symptoms occur as the body attempts to fight off the offending substance and can happen several minutes to several hours after eating the item. These uncomfortable symptoms can cause you to go from irritable to angry in seconds. If you suspect you have a food allergy or want to learn which foods and substances might trigger symptoms like these, speak to your parents, physician, or a nutritionist. They may be able to help you decrease or eliminate these foods or substances from your daily diet.

A final anger irritant is not really a food or a substance. It's about what can happen to your body when the amount of glucose in your blood stream is lower than normal. This condition is hypoglycemia, also called low blood sugar. You may know this as being "hangry." If you feel irritable and jittery when you haven't eaten for a few hours, or in the middle of the night or first thing in the morning, this could mean your blood sugar is too low. So try eating something to see if lightens your mood or helps you feel less dizzy and headachy. If you notice that eating something doesn't help, speak to your physician.

Exercise

If you're like most people, you're not getting as much exercise as you used to get when you were a kid. There are a couple of reasons for this. First, you're busier now than when you were 8 years old. You have more homework and a busier social life. Free time is harder to come by. Another reason teens exercise less is that fewer of them participate in organized sports. While lots of young children participate in organized sports, recent studies have shown that only a very small percentage of them stick with it into their teen years. By high school, sports are more competitive, and teens feel pressured to excel at a sport in order to play. Many decide that competitive sports are not worth the time and stress.

Even though getting regular exercise is tougher now, exercise is still important. A healthy body makes for a healthy mind, and vice versa. Regular aerobic exercise actually changes our brain structure. Along with looking and feeling better and stronger, exercise helps us think more clearly and decreases stress that can trigger anger. Finally, aerobic activity can help your heart pump more efficiently, which can decrease high blood pressure. You might think high blood pressure only happens to adults, but actually, more than four percent of kids and teens have high blood pressure.

Like so many other things, just knowing something is good for us doesn't mean we will do it. Some of us dread exercise and will avoid it at all costs. Exercise doesn't mean you have to run a mile in gym class or swim 50 laps. Aerobic exercise can be fun when it's something that matches your abilities and interests. It can be any physical activity you enjoy that gets your heart pumping. A good workout routine is when you can get thirty minutes of exercise most days.

Have a look at this list and try to pick three to five activities you might enjoy. Then decide when in your daily schedule you can commit to these activities. Be as realistic as possible. It's unlikely you'll be able to take a 30-minute hike in the woods after school as well as attend your piano lesson, tutoring, and family dinner. You just won't have the time or energy to do it all. Kicking the soccer ball around your backyard for 30 minutes might fit better into your schedule.

If you do not see an activity in the list that sounds fun, think of something you enjoy that meets the definition for a cardiovascular workout (thirty minutes of moderate exercise). For example, dodgeball is an aerobic activity and qualifies as exercise. So, too, does dancing in your room for thirty minutes. Get creative!

EXERCISE AND FUN ACTIVITIES

Archery	Horseback Riding	Skiing Cross Country
Badminton	Ice Hockey	Soccer
Basketball	Ice Skating	Softball
Baseball	Jogging	Squash
Bicycling	Jumping Rope	Spin Class
Bowling	Kayaking	Strength Training
Canoeing	Lacrosse	Surfing
Cheerleading	Martial Arts	Swimming
Crew	Mountain Biking	Table Tennis
Curling	Pilates	Tennis
Dancing	Power Lifting	Track and Field
Diving	Racquetball	Ultimate Frisbee
Fencing	Rock Climbing	Volleyball
Field Hockey	Rodeo	Walking
Floor Hockey	Rollerblading	Washing the Car
Football	Rugby	Water Aerobics
Gardening	Running	Water Polo
Golf	Sailing	Weight Lifting
Gymnastics	Scuba Diving	Windsurfing
Handball	Skateboarding	Wrestling
Hiking	Skiing Downhill	Yoga

> Exercise is so boring, and I could never make myself do it. But when I realized that "exercise" doesn't have to mean going to the gym or going for a run, it suddenly seemed possible. I started to dance a little in my room during homework breaks and began to walk our dog more often. I even started to walk a little faster to the bus stop. All these little changes started to add up. I'm feeling healthier, and I'm even thinking of taking a dance class. My best friend takes one, and it might be fun.
> —Camila

Sleep

Everything is harder when you're exhausted. Even little disagreements can become shouting matches when you're tired. Chronic lack of sleep can contribute to declining grades, increased anxiety, impaired athletic performance, and increased risk of motor vehicle accidents. If you're like most teens, you get less than six hours of sleep each night, even though experts say you require at least nine to function optimally. The older you are, the less sleep you tend to get. About one-half of high school seniors go to bed at 11 pm or later on school nights and then must wake up for school at approximately 6:30 am. This amounts to an average of 7.5 hours of sleep per night. Although many teens try to catch up with sleep on weekends, that doesn't help the days you already spent exhausted. And it often makes getting up on Monday even harder than it already is.

Pay Attention to Your Sleep Tank

When you sleep, you fill your sleep tank. As you go through the day, you drain your sleep tank. This means, if you're not getting enough sleep to start with, you begin your days with sleep tanks that are empty (or close to it) and have no opportunity to fill it during the day.

The first step toward improving your sleep is to watch for the warning signs that your sleep tank is chronically low. Place a check mark next to each sign that applies to you. If you checked several of these signs, it's likely you're not getting enough sleep. If you're exhausted most days, speak to your doctor or a sleep specialist, particularly if you snore or have trouble breathing during sleep, experience leg cramps or tingling, or have chronic insomnia even if your sleep habits are good.

SIGNS THAT YOUR SLEEP TANK IS LOW

Trouble waking in the morning and yawning throughout the day.

Trouble getting to school or being late to school on a regular basis.

Reliance on caffeine to remain alert and focused throughout the day.

Trouble staying alert in school, or falling asleep in class.

Feeling more irritable or angry on days when you slept too little.

Napping for more than 45 minutes each day or sleeping in on the weekends for two hours longer than a weekday night.

Keep a Sleep Diary

If you suspect you're not getting enough sleep or you may have a sleep problem, try keeping a sleep diary. Keeping a sleep diary for 2-3 weeks can help you learn your sleep habits, as well as how well and how long you sleep. Once you know how much sleep you get each night and determine the factors that interfere with getting an optimal nine or more hours of sleep nightly, then you can begin to develop a healthy sleep plan.

MY SLEEP DIARY				
Day	Lights-Out Time	Fell Asleep Time	Total Sleep Time (in Minutes)	Fatigue Level (0=Exhausted, 10=Alert)
Monday				
Tuesday				
Wednesday				
Thursday				
Friday				
Saturday				
Sunday				
Instructions: Add your Total Sleep Hours (in minutes) for all seven nights. Take this number and divide it by seven. If you only tracked your sleep pattern for five nights, divide that number by five, etc. Track your sleep for 2-3 weeks if your sleep schedule differs from week to week.				
My average minutes of sleep per night:				

Follow a Consistent Schedule

The single most important thing you can do to sleep well is to go to bed and get out of bed around the same time every day. A standard lights-out time and get-out-of-bed time are the posts that anchor your sleep cycle. Without these posts, your brain doesn't know when to sleep and when to wake up. A confused brain means it's more likely to turn on in the middle of the night because it turned on about that time the night before. Following consistent lights-out and get-out-of bed times is easier said than done for most teens, however, and is particularly difficult during the weekends, when you're accustomed to catching up on your sleep. It's okay to sleep in, but not more than two hours past your usual weekday get-out-of-bed time. If you're willing to follow consist lights-out and out-of-bed times, your sleep will improve in a relatively short time.

Build a Wind-Down Routine

Sleep comes when you signal your mind that you're ready for good sleep. Routines are powerful ways to signal your mind. Creating a wind-down routine that you practice every night is a simple and effective tool to ease your mind toward sleep. Begin your wind-down routine 1–2 hours (or what's feasible) before turning out the lights. Turn off all electronic devices, as the ambient light from screens interferes with your mind's ability to slow down and prepare for sleep. Instead, read a book or magazine, listen to music, take a bath, draw, cuddle with a pet—whatever works for you! It's important you create a wind-down routine that is simple and personal. Try to include things to signal all your senses (sight, sound, taste, smell, touch) that it's time to shift down for sleep.

Practice Good Sleep Habits

The final step toward improving the quantity and quality of your sleep is to eliminate bad sleep habits. Some things may be obvious, such as eliminating caffeine, or cutting back if you try to pack too many academic, social, and extracurricular activities in each day.

HEALTHY SLEEP HABITS

- Keep consistent lights-out and out-of-bed times. These are the guide posts that structure your sleep.

- Try to get at least 8.5 hours of sleep each night, and try for 9.25 hours.

- Transform your room into an environment where going to sleep and staying asleep is easier. Install a light-proof shade or heavy curtains so that your room is dark, or wear an eye mask. Sleep comes as our bodies begin to cool, so make certain your room is nice and cool to help that along. Finally, use a fan to mask noises that might wake you.

- Allow sleep to come naturally. If you cannot fall asleep within 20 minutes, don't fight it. Get out of bed and try a quiet activity such as reading a book or drawing. When you begin to feel drowsy, go back to bed. If you're still awake in 20 minutes, repeat. Eventually, your mind will dim and you will sleep.

- Use your bed for sleep only. Don't watch television, do homework, or talk on the phone in your bed. These activities turn on your mind. When you lay down in bed, you want your mind to know it's time to sleep and begin to turn off.

- Dim the lights at night to signal your mind that it is time for sleep.

- In the morning, turn on the lights and open the blinds and curtains. Light signals your mind that it's time to wake up and start the day.

- It's best to not use televisions, computers, or do homework in your bedroom close to bedtime.

- Set up a regular wind-down routine to signal your mind that it's time for sleep. Take a warm bath or shower. Sip a cup of soothing herbal tea. Read a book or magazine article (paper, not electronic). Listen to music that is calming.

- Do not ingest caffeine (soda, energy drinks, coffee, tea, chocolate) after 1 pm and never to perk up yourself.

- Don't go to bed too hungry or too full. Eat light, nutritious snacks.

- Regular exercise promotes sleep, but complete your workout at least a few hours before lights-out time.

Which of these strategies would you like to try? You might want to ask a parent to help you make some of these changes. If you're interested in learning more about sleep, check the National Sleep Foundation (www.sleepfoundation.org). You'll find up-to-date information about sleep and related topics.

> **"** I created a wind-down routine that is uniquely me. About an hour before lights out, I do a digital-curfew. Phone off, screens off! I sip a cup of warm chamomile tea out of a special mug and listen to relaxing music. I listen to the same couple of songs and use the same mug every night to signal my brain to slow down. I also asked my mom to buy me a new soft plush pillow. When I explained why, she bought one for herself, too. Now we both curl up with the new pillow as part of our wind-down routine. I've been doing this for about three months. Now, as soon as I smell the chamomile tea steeping in the special mug, I can feel my body and mind relax. Sleep is on the way.
> —Camila **"**

You're Angry, Period

Up to half of all women experience physical and psychological symptoms that precede their menstrual cycle, like headaches, water retention and bloating, breast tenderness, increased craving for sweets, depression, moodiness, anxiety and panic, tension, fatigue, forgetfulness, and irritability. For many women, these symptoms occur 5 to 7 days before the onset of their period, but they can begin as early as two weeks prior and can last through the week of their menstrual period. For some women, hormonal changes (an imbalance in estrogen and progesterone) occurring during the second half of the menstrual cycle trigger the onset of irritability or even intense anger when they typically do not experience these symptoms. For other women, these symptoms already exist but worsen during this phase.

If you think you might be experiencing some of these symptoms, use a calendar to monitor your monthly cycle and notice whether your symptoms of Anger (A), Mood (M), and Stress (S) seem to get worse in the days leading up to your period. You can chart each symptom on a scale from 0–10 (0=no symptoms, 10=the worst symptoms ever) on a daily basis (for example, A=3; M=4; S=6). If you observe there is a worsening of these symptoms, the next step is to make some small but significant changes in your eating, exercise, and sleep routines. These changes can help reduce your stress, improve your low mood, and lessen your irritability during the days and weeks leading up to your period.

Start by reducing foods high in sugar, salt, and fat, as well as cutting back on processed foods. Replace those foods with protein, whole grains, and fruits and vegetables. In addition, increase the amount you exercise. Small increases in your exercise level can increase the rate with which your body metabolizes and eliminates toxins that have built up during the month. This is especially important during the seven days prior to your menstrual cycle. Finally, don't cut back on your sleep. Give your body extra rest and get a bit more sleep, if you can, prior to and during your period. Although these suggestions may not eliminate all of the physical and psychological symptoms you experience, they can help reduce the impact on your daily life during the pre-menstrual phase, particularly your level of irritability and your ability to tolerate frustration. If your symptoms are severe, or these suggestions don't help all that much, speak to your physician or gynecologist about your situation.

Develop Your Health Plan

Now that you know more about how eating well, exercising, and getting a good night's sleep can help you manage your anger, you're ready to design your personalized health plan. Use the form below to generate daily and weekly goals to build and maintain healthy nutrition, exercise, and sleep habits.

Life is complicated. A four-day weekend or vacation, or even an outing with friends, can make it difficult to always follow an optimal plan. That's okay. Try to be flexible rather than perfect. If you know in advance you won't be able to eat a balanced diet or cannot avoid high-fat foods for the weekend, for example, because you're staying with Aunt Edna, whose specialty is making fried chicken and biscuits, then plan for it. Eat one piece of fried chicken instead of two. Grab a piece of fruit for a mid-afternoon snack instead of a biscuit and jam. Or, if you can't play a game of basketball because it's raining, consider an indoor activity for exercise. If you can't think of a way to work around a problem, accept that for a few days your meal, exercise, and sleep plans will be less than ideal. Just try to be flexible and get back on track as soon as you can. For example, if lunch is a couple of snacks from the vending machine at school, eat a few more vegetables at dinner. Don't assume a slip is a lost cause. You can always end the day on a good note and get back on track.

MY HEALTH PLAN

NUTRITION

Old Unhealthy Eating Habits:

(*Eat at vending machines; skip meals; eat fast food often; avoid fruits and vegetables, etc.*)

_____

_____

_____

_____

New Healthy Eating Goals:

(*Use rule of thirds; increase my calcium; eat fast food on occasion; more nutritious choices, etc.*)

_____

_____

_____

_____

EXERCISE

Exercise and Fun Activities

List 3-5 activities you enjoy, then track your progress with a check each day you do it.

	Mo	Tu	We	Th	Fr	Sa	Su
_____							
_____							
_____							
_____							
_____							

SLEEP

My current sleep (hours per night): _____

My sleep goal (hours per night): _____

Ideas to improve my sleep: _____

_____

_____

_____

_____

IN A NUTSHELL

Since anger is a mixture of what is going on in your mind *and* what is going on in your body, caring for your body is as important as caring for your mind.

1. Track your eating habits, then begin with small changes. Even small changes in what, when, and how much you eat can result in big changes in your health and stress level. Not only will you look and feel better, but healthy eating calms your emotional system.

2. Try new and fun activities to increase your activity level. Remember, all you need is 30-minutes of moderate aerobic exercise per day. Exercise with friends. The company of good friends will help you get out the door and enjoy the activity more.

3. Sleep is food for the brain and most teens aren't getting enough of it. When you're tired, everything is harder, including managing your anger. A consistent lights-out and out-of-bed time is the most important factor in getting a good night's sleep. Start there and then gradually change your unhelpful sleep habits.

CHAPTER 11

Help, Hope, and Heads-Up

You've covered a lot of territory in this book. You likely started the book beaten down by your anger. You may have believed you were powerless against the speed and power of zero-to-60 anger. By now, however, the story is different. In this book, you've learned about anger and why it can go from zero to 60 in seconds. Perhaps that information alone helped clear your head a little and pointed you in the right direction. As you progressed through the book, you learned several tools to cool the angry body and angry thoughts that fuel your anger. These are important tools and can help most teens get a handle on zero-to-60 anger. You've also learned other important tools, such as communicating clearly, solving problems, and resolving conflicts. These tools can help you manage anger and help you get along with friends, teachers, and parents, and get along in life too.

As you practice these tools over time, you'll notice there are days and perhaps even weeks when you're less angry and more in control of your life. Maybe friends, family, and teachers have noticed and complimented you on the big changes you've made.

Congratulations! It's not easy to handle zero-to-60 anger. It takes time, it takes practice, and most importantly, it takes determination. Even under the best of circumstances, there will be times when you forget what you've learned, and your anger will flare up. All it takes is an unfair situation, or a difficult conversation with a friend, or perhaps a period in which you're feeling stressed and overwhelmed by all the things you have to do. Occasional moments or even periods of anger will happen. It's inevitable. How you handle these slips has a lot to do with whether you continue to improve or fall back into your old angry habits.

In this final chapter, you'll look back over what you've learned and accomplished, and plan your next steps. First, you'll learn about *help*. Some teens benefit from a bit more support and assistance as they learn to handle their zero-to-60 anger. You'll learn when seeking professional help makes sense for you and how to go about doing this. Next, you'll learn about *hope*. Because anger can come and go, it's important to remain hopeful and confident you can continue the progress you've made. Last, you'll learn about *heads-up*. Just because you've learned tools and practiced them doesn't mean your anger won't try to make a comeback. You'll develop a Heads-Up Plan you can use to manage the zero-to-60 anger over the months and years to come.

Help

Many people are experts at helping others. You may be one of them. You help your friends feel better when they're stressed or upset. You help your parents with household chores. You help your younger siblings learn to do things, like ride a bike or shoot a basket. For some, particularly people who've struggled with anger for a while, it's sometimes easier to give help than to ask for it.

Common Reasons People Refuse Help

You might have reasons for why you're not interested in asking for help with anger. Look at the list below to see if any of these apply to you.

It's not my fault. This is perhaps the most common reason teens with zero-to-60 anger give for refusing help. They already feel terrible about anger and often ashamed of what it has done to their friendships and relationships. They may be accustomed to blaming other people rather than accepting their slice of the responsibility pie. It's very difficult to act in ways that affect other people. When you feel terrible about yourself, it can be difficult to ask for help. You may even believe you deserve to suffer because of what your anger has done to other people, and that you must suffer a great deal before it's okay to ask for help. This isn't true. You deserve to feel better, and you're entitled to get help.

I'm too ashamed. Shame makes people want to hide from problems because they've convinced themselves they're bad, or abnormal, or defective. Shame makes it very difficult for people to confess that their lives aren't great and there's a problem. In addition, many people are ashamed by what they've done in the midst of an anger outburst. Perhaps they've yelled at friends and called them names. Perhaps they've convinced themselves that their friends are the problem and have decided to hang out with the other "bad" kids. If you're feeling embarrassed or ashamed about the consequences of the anger, use that to motivate you to do the hard work to change.

It's not that bad. Sometimes people deny there's a problem or minimize just how hard a time they're having with anger. They might compare themselves to family members or friends who get angry from time to time and think, "Hey, my anger isn't as bad as her anger." Different people respond in different ways to anger. You may be coping better than a family member or friend, but you're still suffering. That's reason enough to ask for help.

It's not that bad today. Sometimes people feel angry and sometimes they don't, or at least not as angry as they felt a week ago. Anger fluctuates and often these natural ups and downs can make it difficult to see that anger is really a problem. This is especially true when they're not feeling angry and life is going their way. They think everything is fine. "Why do I need help? I don't have a problem with anger." Just because anger goes up and down doesn't mean it isn't a problem for you. Instead, think about whether anger has been up and down for many months and years, rather than up and down from day to day. Just because anger isn't bad today doesn't mean anger isn't a problem.

What's the point? Some have struggled with zero-to-60 anger for such a long time that they don't believe there's anything that can be done to help them. They're feeling hopeless and depressed, and this only worsens the anger. Perhaps in the past, they've tried to control the anger on their own but weren't able to follow through. Nothing is more demoralizing than trying and trying and never quite succeeding. After a while, they give up. But just because you haven't been successful on your own doesn't mean you can't be successful if you have a little help and the right tools—like those in this book. Anger is a difficult problem, and many people benefit from professional help.

Although it might be difficult to accept help, it's okay to ask for it. Everyone asks for help. A musician might ask for an extra rehearsal, or sit in with another musician to warm up, or get some support before a performance or a recording session. An actor might consult with a dialect coach to prepare for a new role in a movie or television show. A professional basketball player might ask a teammate for help with his jump shot. If you're willing to ask for help with anger, it's likely you'll solve the anger problem. Asking for help is an important first step for many, and once you decide to ask for help, or at least consider the possibility, you're on your way to an easier and better life.

> 66 It was really hard for me to tell my mom that I wanted to meet with a therapist. I felt bad about the ways I've treated my mom, my brother, and my friends because I couldn't cool down. I kept making excuses and blaming people. They were mean to me. They didn't treat me fairly. They didn't really care about me. Even though I said all those things, I knew that anger was the real problem. Once I told my mom that I wanted help, I started to feel better. She told me that it wasn't my fault that I got so angry, but just because it wasn't my fault didn't mean that it wasn't my job to learn to handle it. I know she's right. She told me that she was very proud of me for taking this first step. I'm kind of proud of me too.
>
> —Emma 99

Is It Time for Professional Help?

Sometimes in life we could use a little help, and typically we know when we need it. We also tend to know who can help us and how to get help from this person. For example, learning to drive is a time when you could use some help. That help usually comes from an adult who goes with you to get your drivers permit and then teaches you how to drive. It's difficult to learn to drive without help of some kind. Similarly, if you catch a cold, you know to ask your mom to call your doctor. If you're struggling with a math problem, you know to ask your teacher or a friend for help.

When you're dealing with anger, you might think you have to manage things on your own. It doesn't occur to you that asking for help might be a good thing. Do any of these phrases sound familiar? "I can manage it," "I've got it," "I wouldn't have a problem with anger if you were just nice to me." If you're like most people, you probably want to do things without help from others. You want to take charge of your life and show parents, teachers, and other adults you can take care of yourself. Refusing help and doing it alone might work okay for certain problems, such as a homework assignment, but if anger is making your life hard, getting some help may be the smart thing to do. It might be time for professional help if:

- you're not getting significantly better.
- you're having trouble setting aside time to practice the skills.
- you've worked on anger for a while, but you're now feeling down and hopeless that things can change for you.
- you have depression, anxiety, or alcohol or drug use that makes it hard for you to practice the tools in this book.
- you're overwhelmed by the day-to-day stress of life, or if life has become so complicated that it's difficult to get through the day.

REASONS THE ANGER ENGINE STILL RUNS HOT	
Problem	**Fix**
Your goals weren't realistic. If you're like most people, the tools you've learned have improved things for you. However, although you're progressing, it's not realistic to expect that you won't have bumps. You're changing a habit of thinking and acting, and, like any habit, it takes time and you'll slip back into those old patterns from time to time. It's important that you're realistic about your progress. If you overreact to a slip, you can lose confidence and then give up too soon.	Don't jump to conclusions. Don't assume that falling back into the old anger habits for a moment means that you're not improving and that the tools aren't working. Don't be hard on yourself for the natural ups and downs of getting better. You know the old saying, "Get back on the horse that threw you." That's a great approach for working on anything that's difficult, such as cooling the anger engine. When anger pops back into your life, don't criticize yourself. Instead, get back on the horse that threw you as soon as you can. Also, remember that anger is natural and will never go away completely. A realistic goal is to accept that the anger engine will rev from time to time, and your job is to use the tools before the anger gets out of hand.
You didn't practice enough. Learning to cool the anger engine takes time and practice. Many people don't improve quickly because they haven't practiced the skills enough. You may have read all the chapters but not practiced the skills, or practiced but not enough to build a new mental engine or habit. Remember, it takes a lot of practice for new skills to become automatic and natural.	If you didn't put in enough practice time, give it another try. First, re-read Chapter 2 (Reflect and Record) to remind yourself of the consequences of not working to cool the anger engine. This will motivate you again to work hard and practice the tools. Then, re-read the chapters that describe the easiest tools to learn and practice, such as deep slow breathing, or muscle relaxation. This will get you back into the practice habit.

Your life is too busy and too complicated. Learning and practicing new skills takes time. Some people are too busy to find another moment to do anything else. They run from one activity to the next: school work, soccer practice, friends, and family events. It's hard to find the time or energy to work on your anger.	Although you want to learn tools to cool the anger engine, you might not have the time, energy, or calmness in your life to do what's necessary to make this happen. If this is you, consider seeking help from a mental health professional. Often, a little more support can make a big difference. Also, a psychotherapist can help you sort through your life complications and help you solve some of the problems that make it tough for you improve on your own.
You have other problems that anger is masking. Lots of people who struggle with anger struggle with other problems too: depression, anxiety, learning difficulties, family problems, or alcohol and drugs. If any of these problems are serious, it can make it very difficult for you to achieve your goal of learning to cool the anger engine.	It may be time for you to meet with a psychotherapist. Not only will you feel better with a little more support, the psychotherapist can help you with other problems, such as depression or anxiety. Also, the psychotherapist might recommend a medication to help you, too. It's difficult to make much progress on solving any problem, and particularly an anger problem, when you're very depressed. You can also check the self-help books in the resource section of this book. They may give you a few ideas that will help.

How could a psychotherapist help? It's not easy to overcome zero-to-60 anger, and a psychotherapist can really help. Sometimes all it takes is a little reminder or a word of encouragement to get the ball rolling and keep it rolling. A psychotherapist can help you practice the tools in this book or help you select or modify the tools that are likely to help you the most. A psychotherapist can gently nudge you toward trying hard things, while being patient and supportive along the way. Also, it's great to have a sounding board; not everything that makes you angry is because of you. Everyone feels a little angry, and it helps to get some support and advice from a neutral party who knows you and whom you trust.

Meeting with a psychotherapist is particularly important if you're struggling with depression, anxiety, or panic attacks, or if things are difficult at home. If you're not in psychotherapy, but would like to try it, talk to your parents.

What kind of professional could help? When it comes to selecting a mental health professional with whom to meet, it's a bit of an alphabet soup. There's LPC, EdD, LCSW, MFT, MD, PhD, PsyD. What do all those letters mean? Agreeing to meet with a professional can feel scary, especially when you see all those letters. Don't worry, the letters are just the professionals telling the public about their training and what they can do to help. Some professionals have gone to medical school, just like your pediatrician, except their area of specialty is in something called psychiatric medicine. They're a doctor, and their letters are MD, which stands for Medical Doctor. Other professionals are also called "doctor," but they didn't go to medical school. These people have achieved the highest level of training in their area of specialty and have received a Doctorate degree. For example, psychologists or educational psychologists have letters like PhD, PsyD, or EdD. Finally, there are therapists trained specifically to provide counseling, and these people have a Master's degree in social work or psychology, such as licensed clinical social workers (LCSW), marriage and family therapists (MFT), or licensed professional counselors (LPC). All these professionals are trained to treat typical mental health problems. At the same time, certain mental health professionals specialize in particular problems, such as alcohol or drug problems, or anxiety disorders. Any one of these professionals can likely help you with anger or problems that anger might be masking, such as anxiety or depression.

Find a professional. Most people feel anxious when they first meet with a psychotherapist, particularly if they've never discussed their anger with someone they don't know. Many have second thoughts about coming in to see a psychotherapist for the first time, or have doubts psychotherapy can help them. Try not to let your second thoughts stand in the way of getting help. Working with a psychotherapist who can teach you practical and effective tools—like the tools described in this book—can be an important part of the plan to help you learn to manage your anger.

To lessen some of the anxiety you might have about starting psychotherapy, you'll want to know the person is the right psychotherapist to help you. Look at the list below. At the first meeting, it's okay to ask the psychotherapist whether they have the qualifications to help you with your anger. In addition, it's important that you feel comfortable with the person and clearly understand your role and the psychotherapist's role in helping you. To ensure the psychotherapist is qualified to help you, make certain they:

- Have professional training in medicine, counseling, or psychology.
- Have experience working with adolescents.
- Have experience treating mental health issues, such as anger, but also anxiety and depression.
- Will keep information you share confidential, unless they think that you might hurt yourself or other people, or if someone is hurting you.
- Will help you to set therapy goals that are realistic and make sense to you.
- Is open to your feedback if the psychotherapy isn't helping.

Once you've decided you're ready to start psychotherapy, you'll want to locate a trained mental health professional. If you live in a large city or densely populated area, it'll likely be easy for you to find a qualified mental health professional to help. However, if you live in a rural area or small community, it may be a bit more difficult. Here are some tips that can help you find the right person:

- Talk to your pediatrician or school counselor for a referral to a psychotherapist.
- Call your insurance company for a referral to a psychotherapist on your insurance panel.
- Ask adults you trust (parents, teachers, school counselors, parents of a friend) for the name of a psychotherapist in your community.
- Ask a friend who has met with a psychotherapist for a suggestion, or ask a friend who is in psychotherapy to ask his or her therapist for a recommendation.
- Use online resources to find therapists in your community, such as the following:

- American Psychological Association: www.apa.org
- Association for Behavioral and Cognitive Therapies: www.abct.org
- Academy of Cognitive Therapy: www.academyofct.org
- Anxiety and Depression Association of America: www.adaa.org
- Beck Institute of Cognitive Behavior Therapy: www.beckinstitute.org
- Psychology Today: www.psychologytoday.com

66 It took me a long time to work up the courage to ask to see a psychotherapist. I was too embarrassed. I thought seeing a shrink meant that I was crazy. And I didn't really want to tell a stranger my personal business. They don't know me! But trying to fix my anger on my own wasn't working. Not enough, anyway. Eventually I decided to ask my parents if I could meet with a doctor. I'm glad I did. I needed the extra help. This doctor was more like a coach than a doctor. Turns out sometimes having someone that doesn't know me can actually be a good thing—I don't have to worry about her judging me, or being disappointed in me, or about ruining my relationship with her. Her help has really made a difference.
—Jamal 99

Prepare to meet with the professional. Many people who are considering psychotherapy for the first time are often uncertain about what to expect during the first meeting. Don't assume psychotherapy and psychotherapists all look and act like what you see on television or in the movies. Although entertaining, these are actors are not real therapists, and psychotherapy almost never looks like what you see on television. Also, it might take several tries before you find the right psychotherapist. They're people too, and you may click with one person but not another. That's totally fine.

Q&A Time

Now that you know more about who these professionals are, you probably have some questions. The following are frequently asked questions teens have when they first meet with me, and they've given permission for me to share them with you.

QUESTION

Will I have to take tests or have a physical exam for the doctor to know what's wrong with me?

ANSWER

Probably not. Some doctors or psychotherapists might want you to fill out questionnaires to help them understand more about you and your situation. Other doctors or psychotherapists might prefer to gather this information simply by asking you questions and taking notes, like an interview. Obtaining this information helps them to understand the problem and then recommend the best treatment plan for you. Sometimes, however, your doctor is a psychiatrist who can prescribe medication. Before the psychiatrist gives you any medication, they might refer you for some medical tests or to give you a physical exam (like listening to your heart and lungs) to determine whether you're healthy and to make sure there isn't a medical reason for the problem. These steps ensure the psychiatrist can safely prescribe medication to you.

QUESTION

Will the doctor tell my parents, teachers, or other people what I say?

ANSWER

There is a term called confidentiality, or privacy, which protects the information a client shares with a psychotherapist. However, because you're a minor until you turn 18, your parents have the legal right to talk to your doctor without your consent or permission. Therefore, it's important to discuss this with your parents and the psychotherapist when you start psychotherapy. You can decide together what information is private between you and your psychotherapist, and what information the psychotherapist can share with your parents, teachers, or your pediatrician.

QUESTION

Will I have to take medication?

ANSWER

Some doctors might recommend you take medication in addition to counseling or psychotherapy. For some people, anger masks other problems or conditions, such as depression, and medications can help you feel less depressed. However, talk this over with your doctor and your parents. It's important that you understand why the doctor is recommending medication in addition to psychotherapy.

QUESTION

How long do I have to meet with the psychotherapist or doctor?

ANSWER

The number of meetings can vary from a few (fewer than 10 sessions), to many (20 sessions or more). You and the psychotherapist will decide how long to meet based on your specific situation and how the anger affects your life, as well as what you want to accomplish in your psychotherapy.

QUESTION

What if I don't like the psychotherapist?

ANSWER

This can happen! Hopefully, you'll like your person enough to meet a few times to see whether you're comfortable working with them. However, if after several meetings you really don't click with the therapist, talk to your parents or even to the therapist. Together you can figure out whether it's best for you to work with someone else.

QUESTION

What makes a psychotherapist better able to help me than someone I already know and trust?

ANSWER

Although people you know and trust, and even love, can be a great support when you're struggling, they sometimes have other roles and responsibilities that can get in the way of them being fully available to you. In addition, it's not easy for a friend or parent to be completely objective when it comes to advising you. The job of the psychotherapist is to place your interests and well-being first and to be as objective as they can in advising you. In addition, a psychotherapist experienced in helping teens will know which tools and what kind of advice are the most effective in helping cool the anger. Friends or parents, although well-meaning, can sometimes suggest things that actually make the anger worse.

Hope

Hope is believing things will work out. Nothing builds hope more than success. Take a few minutes now and review what you've learned and the tools that have helped the most to cool your anger. Perhaps over the last few weeks and months you've used some of the tools to stay cool in a difficult conversation or when someone accused you of something you didn't do. Perhaps you used the assertiveness tool to ask someone to stop, and the person stopped. Perhaps you reacted calmly in a situation because you've been practicing the cool body tools, and your body was relaxed. Perhaps the tools have helped decrease the frequency and intensity of your anger outbursts. Perhaps you're managing your relationships with friends, teachers, and your parents a little better, and you're feeling more hopeful things will work out okay there, too. Congratulations! It's not easy to cool your anger. Each step, each small success builds confidence in the skills you've learned and in yourself. It's important to remember your successes in order to remain confident and hopeful. Dealing with your anger is a bumpy road, and there will be ups and downs. A hopeful approach will help you stick to the path you're on to cool your anger.

If you're unsure whether things are better, ask a parent or friend if they've noticed any changes. (You don't need to tell them you were using the book.) Ask them, "Do I seem a little less irritable or angry to you? Have you seen me trying to keep cool? Do I seem a little more positive?" Reward yourself for what you've accomplished. The reward can be a simple pat on the back: "I've worked hard, and it wasn't easy. I'm pleased with what I accomplished." Alternatively, you might schedule a fun activity with your family or a friend to celebrate.

Heads-Up

Now that you've learned to handle your anger and your life is back on track, you'll want to have a plan to stay on track. This is your Heads-Up Plan. Heads-up means watching for anger to make a comeback—and it will come back, at least in fits and starts. No matter how successful you've been, it's essential you stay alert for the first signs of anger. This is the heads-up attitude to anger. If you're prepared for an anger comeback, you're more likely to respond with the tools you've learned.

Your Heads-Up Plan has three parts:

- Anger early warning signs.
- Tools you've used to cool the anger.
- Typical anger risks and remedies.

Anger Early Warning Signs

The first step in building your Heads-Up Plan is to identify the early warning signs of anger. Because anger is normal, you'll feel angry from time to time. That's okay, so long as you quickly recognize the signs that you've slipped into old angry patterns and then quickly use the tools you've learned to get back on track. Perhaps it's a feeling in your body, such as clenching your jaw. Perhaps it's a particular angry thought or image, such as imagining you're hitting someone in the face. Perhaps it's an old habit, such as not asserting yourself. Although it's not always easy to recognize you've fallen back into old angry habits, the key is to look out for the first signs that your anger is starting to warm. The anger early warning signs include:

- Typical situations that provoke anger outbursts.
- Typical angry body signals.
- Typical angry thoughts.
- Typical angry actions (including the drumbeat of anger).
- Typical problems created by anger.

Look at Jason's list of anger early warning signs. Then, take a few minutes and on a blank sheet of paper, write your anger early warning signs. Look once more at the ABCs of Anger forms you've completed. All your anger early warning signs are there.

JASON'S ANGER EARLY WARNING SIGNS

Typical anger triggers (people, situations).	My dad telling me what to do.
	People who act like they know it all.
	Mr. Smith, my social studies teacher.
	Unfair situations.
Typical angry body signals.	Make fists with my hands.
	Face is hot.
	Sneering and squinting my eyes.
	Tight arms and shoulders.
Typical angry thoughts and images.	Imagining hitting someone in the face.
	Urge to yell.
	Thinking: "That's completely unfair."
	Thinking: "You did it on purpose."

Typical angry actions.	Screaming at them and calling them jerks.
	Thinking about what the person did over and over.
	Walking past people and shoving them with my shoulder.
Typical problems created by anger.	My dad grounds me for the weekend.
	My dad won't take me to soccer practice or the games.
	Mr. Smith gives me more homework.
	I get sent home and miss important stuff in class so I can't do the homework.
	I lose friends or my best friend won't hang out with me for a few days and I have to sit alone at lunch.

Anger Cycle and Tools

The next step in building your Heads-Up Plan is to list the tools you've learned and practiced. Remember, anger outbursts include three parts: angry body, angry thoughts, and angry actions. You've learned tools for each of these parts. For example, you've learned tools to cool your angry body and tools to cool your angry thoughts. You probably have a favorite tool or two now, but make certain to consider all the tools you've learned, not just the ones that are your go-to tools. The more tools you have that work for you, the more confident you'll feel in new and unusual situations.

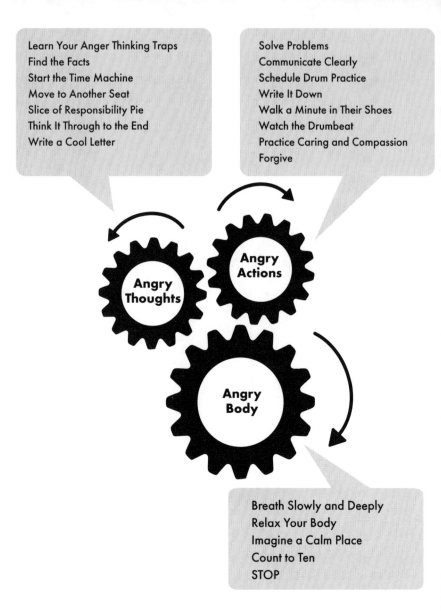

Learn Your Anger Thinking Traps
Find the Facts
Start the Time Machine
Move to Another Seat
Slice of Responsibility Pie
Think It Through to the End
Write a Cool Letter

Solve Problems
Communicate Clearly
Schedule Drum Practice
Write It Down
Walk a Minute in Their Shoes
Watch the Drumbeat
Practice Caring and Compassion
Forgive

Angry Thoughts

Angry Actions

Angry Body

Breath Slowly and Deeply
Relax Your Body
Imagine a Calm Place
Count to Ten
STOP

Know Your Risks and Remedies

You've likely noticed certain situations, interactions, and people make you angry. You can't avoid these events. They're part of life. The best you can do is prepare for them. Knowing which events and people provoke anger outbursts helps you prepare for them.

These are the risks. The tools you've learned, particularly the ones that have worked the best to cool anger outbursts, are the remedies.

Look at the ABCs of Anger forms you completed as you worked through this book. Think about the situations in the A column. Is there a kid or teacher at school who pushes your buttons? Is stress a risk? Do you feel angry and irritable before a big exam or during big changes, such as moving to a new school or neighborhood? Are new people or situations a risk? Do you see any of those on your ABCs of Anger forms? On a blank piece of paper, write all the risks you see on the ABCs of Anger forms and from other situations or people that make you angry.

Next, think through the tools you've learned in this book. These are the remedies. Some readers work from beginning of the book to end, while others jump around, trying tools they think will work best for their particular situations. Either way, you probably have your favorites. Perhaps you like the deep calming breaths and use them often. Or, perhaps you like to say a few calming thoughts to yourself. As teens learn and practice the tools in this book, their lives become calmer and less complicated. That's when they might temporarily stop using the tools, and then anger might become a problem again. The good news is you can turn things around pretty quickly once you start using the tools again. Now, look at the list of typical risks and remedies and note the risks that are the big ones for you. Then, write the numbers for the remedies you've used the most and are likely to use again.

Build Your Heads-Up Plan

Now it's time to build your Heads-Up Plan. Your Heads-Up Plan will include all the important information and tools you've

Cool Body Remedies or Tools

1	Breathe slowly and deeply.	2	Relax your body.
3	Imagine a calm place.	4	STOP and count to ten.

Cool Thinking Tools

5	Find the facts.	6	Start the time machine.
7	Move to another seat.	8	Share a slice of the responsibility pie.
9	Think it through to the end.	10	_____

Stop the Drum Beat Tools

11	Schedule drum practice.	12	Distract yourself.
13	Laugh a little.	14	Write it down.
15	Walk a minute in their shoes.	16	Savor the good and pleasant.
17	Watch the drum beat of anger.	18	Find the good things in someone.
19	Practice care and compassion toward self.	20	Forgive.

Other Action Tools

21	Express anger effectively.	22	Listen actively.
23	Stand up for yourself.	24	Take feedback effectively.
25	Negotiate a compromise.	26	De-escalate conflict.
27	ICCAN	28	_____

Risk	**Remedy**
_____	_____
_____	_____
_____	_____
_____	_____
_____	_____
_____	_____
_____	_____
_____	_____

learned in this book. If you've felt cool and calm without the roar of anger for many weeks or months, you may not have thought about these tools or considered which tools helped cool anger outbursts the most. That's okay. It's best to build your plan when you're cool, calm, and thinking clearly. That way, when anger does strike again, you're more likely to believe the wise things you wrote.

Once you've built your Heads-Up Plan, you might share it with a parent or even your counselor or psychotherapist if you're comfortable doing so. If in the future you start to notice zero-to-60 anger is trying to make a comeback, it helps if those who want to help you know just how to do it. Your Heads-Up Plan lays it all out for them. Although it may be tempting to toss the Heads-Up Plan into your desk drawer or stuff it in a book, I encourage you to keep it where you can find it when you need it. You might even tell your support people where you keep your plan so that they can find it if you want help.

Look at Jason's Heads-Up Plan. His plan will give you an idea of what yours might look like. Remember, this is your Heads-Up Plan. Everyone's plan will look a little different. That's the point, really. The more personal the plan, the more likely it'll be to alert you to the first signs of anger. Also, you might not like certain tools. They might have felt too awkward to use repeatedly, or certain tools might not work well for you. That's okay. Just make note of those tools that are your favorites. If you don't remember a particular tool or how it works to calm your angry thoughts, just take a mini-refresher course and re-read the description of the tool. In the blank My Heads-Up Plan at the end of this chapter, follow these steps to build your own Heads-Up Plan:

1. Circle all your angry body and angry thinking warning signs and add any that aren't listed.

2. Circle your favorite cool body and cool thinking tools and add any that aren't listed.

3. Circle your favorite action tools and add any that aren't listed.

4. List several encouragement thoughts. These are usually encouraging phrases or inspiring words. They'll help you to stick it out when things get difficult or complicated.

5. Last, add other important points or tips you learned and want to remember.

JASON'S HEADS-UP PLAN

Angry Body Early Warning Signs

(Feeling like your face and neck are hot.)	(Corners of mouth are turned down)
Grinding your teeth.	Sweating.
Breathing heavily.	(Neck and shoulders are tense and tight.)
Trembling.	Feeling nauseated.
(Hands and arms are tense.)	Head throbbing.
Grimacing.	Crying.
Looking down.	Breathing heavily.
Shaking my head.	Making fists.

Angry Thoughts Early Warning Signs

("I hate you.")	("That's not fair.")
"Shut up."	"I didn't do it."
("I want to hit you.")	"Get away from me."
"Don't mess with me."	"You don't care about me."
"Back off."	"I'll show you."
"You did it on purpose."	"You're not listening to me."
("I hate you.")	"You always do that."
"Get out of my face."	"You're a control freak!"

My Typical Thinking Traps

Jumping to conclusions.

Binocular vision.

Fallacy of fairness.

The line.

Shoulds, need-tos, and have-tos.

Black-or-white.

Fortune telling.

Mind reading.

Overgeneralization.

End of the world.

Need to be right.

My Favorite Cool Thoughts Tools

Find the facts.

Share a slice of the responsibility pie.

Start the time machine.

Think it through to the end.

Move to another seat.

My Favorite Cool Body Tools

Breathe slowly and deeply.

Relax your body.

Imagine a calm place.

STOP and count to ten.

My Favorite Action Tools

My Favorite Drum Beat Tools

Schedule drum practice.

Distract yourself.

Laugh a little.

Write it down rather than beat the drum.

Walk a minute in their shoes.

Savor the good and pleasant.

Surf the drum beat of anger.

Find the good things in someone.

Practice care and compassion toward yourself.

Forgive.

My Favorite Other Action Tools

Express anger effectively.

Listen actively.

Stand up for yourself.

Take feedback effectively.

Negotiate a compromise.

De-escalate conflict.

ICCAN

Encouragement Thoughts

Cooling down isn't easy but you can do it. Take a couple of calming breaths. It's not that bad.

Your friends are noticing that you're nicer and calmer. Keep up the great work!

Other Important Things to Remember

People aren't really out to get you. That's just something that your mind jumps to when you're angry.

Most times you're angry because someone hurt your feelings. Tell them they hurt your feelings rather than yelling at them.

Make an Appointment With Yourself to Practice

Just like most of the things you've learned—basketball, gymnastics, swimming, soccer—practicing at least periodically is the way you get and stay good at it. Managing zero-to-60 anger is no different. Practice is the key to staying in shape and staying in shape takes some work and effort on your part. It pays to practice a little every day or week. That will be easy with some tools, like slow deep breathing, or imagining a positive place. Other tools may take a bit more time, such as preparing to be assertive with a friend or teacher. The key is practice. Set aside 10–20 minutes once a week for the next six months and then once a month for the following six months and do the following:

- Review your Heads-Up Plan.
- Identify potential stressors coming up for you and think through the tools you'll use to handle these.
- Plan your nutrition, exercise, and sleep goals for the upcoming week.
- Practice your slow deep breathing, progressive muscle relaxation, or positive imagery tools every night, particularly if you're in a prolonged period of stress. Remember, a tense body makes anger flare before you know it.
- At least once or twice each week, sit down and complete an ABCs of Anger form. In order to handle anger, it's very important to keep your eye on all the parts: angry body, angry thoughts, and angry actions. Recording your anger outbursts will help you do this.

Although at first it might seem like a lot of work, scheduling a regular check-in with yourself, as well as regularly using your favorite tools, will build a strong practice habit. It's no different than building the habit of brushing your teeth every night before bed, or doing homework. The people who are most successful in handling zero-to-60 anger are the ones who develop a realistic and consistent practice plan.

> I'm headed to college in the fall, and I'm really excited, but it's also a big change. Change really stresses me out, and when I'm stressed, I get irritable. I have this in my Heads-Up Plan along with a list of my favorite tools. The problem-solving tool is a big one for me, and being assertive is, too. I've practiced these tools a lot over the last few months, and I'm much calmer these days. I plan to read through my Heads-Up Plan once a week. It only takes a few minutes, and it's worth reminding myself of my early warning signs and the tools that helped me cool my anger engine.
>
> —Jamal

IN A NUTSHELL

If you're like most people with zero-to-60 anger, anger took up a lot of space in your life. Life was complicated and, frankly, not a lot of fun. You're on your way to an easier life with more space to become the person you want to be (and deep down, truly are). The tools in this book will help you continue.

1. Learning to cool zero-to-60 anger isn't easy, and you don't have to do it alone. It's okay to ask for help. If you've tried the tools in this book and your anger is still out of control, it may be time to meet with a counselor or psychotherapist. A caring ear and a little support can make all the difference in the world for you.

2. There will be ups and downs, and during the downs you may wonder if you can do this. Remember, hope is believing things will work out, and nothing builds hope more than success. Set realistic goals and don't be hard on yourself if you slip back into old anger habits. Practice and persistence are the key.

3. No matter how successful you've been, it's essential that you stay alert for the first sign of anger so you can respond with the tools you've learned. Your Heads-Up Plan will help you.

Remember, from time to time, we all rent space to anger. Doctors, engineers, and professional athletes, adults from every walk of life, all have angry moments, perhaps even an angry day. Anger doesn't mean you can't succeed, as long as you have the tools to handle it. You can have friends, go to a good college, and one day have a good job. You can have all these things and more, as long as you know how to keep your cool. Good luck!

MY HEADS-UP PLAN

Angry Body Early Warning Signs

Feeling like your face and neck are hot.

Grinding your teeth.

Breathing heavily.

Trembling.

Hands and arms are tense.

Grimacing.

Looking down.

Corners of mouth are turned down.

Sweating.

Neck and shoulders are tense and tight.

Feeling nauseated.

Head throbbing.

Crying.

Breathing heavily.

_____

_____

_____

_____

Angry Thoughts Early Warning Signs

"I hate you."

"Shut up."

"I want to hit you."

"Don't mess with me."

"Back off."

"You did it on purpose."

"I hate you."

"That's not fair."

"I didn't do it."

"Get away from me."

"You don't care about me."

"I'll show you."

"You're not listening to me."

"You always do that."

_____

_____

_____

_____

My Favorite Cool Body Tools

Breathe slowly and deeply.

Imagine a calm place.

Relax your body.

STOP and count to ten.

My Typical Thinking Traps

Jumping to conclusions.

Fallacy of fairness.

Shoulds, need-tos, and have-tos.

Fortune telling.

Overgeneralization.

Need to be right.

Binocular vision.

The line.

Black-or-white.

Mind reading.

End of the world.

My Favorite Cool Thoughts Tools

Find the facts.

Start the time machine.

Move to another seat.

Share a slice of the responsibility pie.

Think it through to the end.

My Favorite Action Tools

My Favorite Stop the Drum Beat Tools

Schedule drum practice.

Distract yourself.

Laugh a little.

Write It down rather than beat the drum.

Walk a minute in their shoes.

Savor the good and pleasant.

Surf the drum beat of anger.

Find the good things in someone.

Practice care and compassion toward yourself.

Forgive.

My Favorite Other Action Tools

Express anger effectively.

Listen actively.

Stand up for yourself.

Take feedback effectively.

Negotiate a compromise.

De-escalate conflict.

ICCAN

Encouragement Thoughts

_____   _____

_____   _____

_____   _____

_____   _____

Other Important Things to Remember

_____   _____

_____   _____

_____   _____

_____   _____

RESOURCES

Readings for Teens

Hansen, S. A. (2013). *The executive functioning workbook for teens: Help for unprepared, late and scattered teens*. New Harbinger Publications.

Honos-Webb, L. (2011). *The ADHD workbook for teens*. New Harbinger Publications.

Knauss, W. 2016. *Overcoming procrastination for teens: A CBT guide for college-bound students*. New Harbinger Publications.

Quinn, P. O., & Maitland, T. E. L. (2011). *On your own: A college readiness guide for teens with ADHD/LD*. Magination Press.

Sisemore, T. A. (2010). *Free from OCD: A workbook for teens with obsessive-compulsive disorder*. New Harbinger Publications.

Skeen, M., McKay, M., Fanning, P. & Skeen, K. (2016). *Communication skills for teens*. New Harbinger Publications.

Tompkins, M. A., & Barkin, J. R. (2018). *The relaxation and stress reduction workbook for teens: CBT skills to help you deal with worry and anxiety*. New Harbinger Publications.

Tompkins, M. A., & Martinez, K. (2009). *My anxious mind: A teen's guide to managing anxiety and panic*. Magination Press.

Tompkins, M. A., & Thompson, M. Q. (2018). *The insomnia workbook for teens: Skills to help you stop stressing and start sleeping better*. New Harbinger Publications.

Toner, J. B., & Freeland, C. A. B. (2016). *Depression: A teen's guide to survive and thrive*. Magination Press.

Readings for Parents

Anxiety

Achar Josephs, S. (2017). *Helping your anxious teen: Positive parenting strategies to help your teen beat anxiety, stress, and worry.* New Harbinger Publications.

Chansky, T. E. (2014). *Freeing your child from anxiety: Practical strategies to overcome fears, worries, and phobias and be prepared for life — from toddlers to teens.* Harmony.

Attention-Deficit Hyperactivity Disorder

Barkley, R. A. (2013). *Taking charge of ADHD: The complete authoritative guide for parents (3rd ed.).* Guilford Press.

Guare, R., & Dawson, P. (2012). *Smart but scattered teens: The "executive skills" program for helping teens reach their potential.* Guilford Press.

Depression

Mondimore, F. M., & Kelly, P. (2015). *Adolescent depression: A guide for parents.* John Hopkins University Press.

Medication

Wilens, T. E., & Hammerness, P. G. (2016). *Straight talk about psychiatric medications for kids (4th ed.).* Guilford Press.

Online Resources

Cognitive Behavioral Therapy

The following associations provide teens and parents with qualified mental health professionals who specialize in cognitive behavioral therapy for a variety of problems, such as anxiety, anger, and depression:

Academy of Cognitive Therapy
www.academyofct.org

Association for Behavioral and Cognitive Therapies
www.abct.org

Anxiety and Depression Association of America
www.adaa.org

Beck Institute for Cognitive Behavior Therapy
www.beckinstitute.org

International OCD Foundation
www.iocdf.org

Professional Associations
The following professional associations provide teens and parents with brochures, tips, and articles on the psychological and emotional issues that affect a person's physical and emotional well-being:

American Academy of Child and Adolescent Psychiatry
www.aacap.org

American Psychiatric Association
www.psych.org

American Psychological Association
www.apa.org

Sleep
The following websites provide information to professionals and the public on sleep disorders, sleep hygiene, sleep treatments and accredited sleep laboratories and centers in their area:

American Academy of Sleep Medicine
www.aasmnet.org

American Insomnia Association
www.americaninsomniaassociation.org

National Sleep Foundation (NSF)
www.sleepfoundation.org

Bullying
The following websites provide information and videos to professionals and the public on bullying and resources and strategies to intervene to assist teens who are bullied:

National Bullying Prevention Center
www.pacer.org/bullying

PREVNet Bullying Prevention Program
www.prevnet.ca

Stop Bullying Now
www.stopbullyingnow.com

Trauma

The following websites provide information to professionals and the public on trauma, and childhood abuse:

Allegheny General Hospital
Center for Traumatic Stress in Children and Adolescents
www.ahn.org/specialties/mental-health/ctsca

American Professional Society on the Abuse of Children
www.apsac.org

CARES (Child Abuse Research Education Service) Institute
www.caresinstitute.org

International Society for Traumatic Stress Studies
www.istss.org

Medical University of South Carolina
National Crime Victims Research and Treatment Center
www.musc.edu/cvc

National Child Traumatic Stress Network
www.nctsnet.org

Health Information

The following U.S. government websites provide information on physical and mental health:

Food and Drug Administration (FDA)
www.fda.gov

National Institutes of Health (NIH)
www.nih.gov

National Institute of Mental Health (NIMH)
www.nimh.nih.gov

Mobile Apps

Breath2Relax. Learn and practice diaphragmatic breathing and detailed information on the effects of stress on the body.

Happify. Learn and practice activities that can help you combat negativity, anxiety, and stress while fostering positive traits like gratitude and empathy.

Headspace. Learn and practice a series of guided meditations and mindfulness exercises.

My Mood Tracker. Helps you track your mood. As you become more aware of what you're feeling when, you can begin to figure out links between life events and cycles and your moods, which in turn will help you manage (and work around) your moods.

Pay It Forward. Learn and practice a daily act of kindness—a proven stress reducer—with a list of suggestions. Get a connection to a community of people who are committed to the principles of paying it forward.

The Mindfulness App. Learn and practice five guided meditations, with options for listening to calming music or nature sounds.

INDEX

ABCs of Anger, 11–29, 37
   in anger cycle, 18–19
   and anger thermometer, 27–29
   anger thinking traps and, 68
   Antecedents, 12–13
   Basics of Anger, 13–16
   Consequences, 16–18
   Cool Thinking tools with, 88
   defusing conflict with, 151
   Hassle Plans based on, 164
   identifying body's anger signals
    from, 19–27
   practice with, 246
   recording, 17
   risks of anger and, 242
Academy of Cognitive Therapy,
   234, 256
Acceptance. *See also* Self-
   acceptance of compliments, 175
   defusing conflict with, 150
   with forgiveness, 108–110
Accomplishments
   exaggerating, 177
   over-focusing on, 173
   rewarding yourself for, 238
   tearing down others', 177
Accusations. *See also* Conflict
   false, 157–159
   as part of life, 147
   true, 158–163
Achievement, as core value, 35
Acknowledgment, in forgiveness,
   110
Acting, before thinking, 84, 86–87
Actions, angry. *See also* Drumbeat
   of anger

   in anger cycle, 19
   angry thoughts as fuel for, 53
   in Basics of Anger, 12, 15–16
   as early warning signal, 239
   minuses of, 30–33
   pluses of, 33
   possible solutions involving, 141
   practicing tools to calm, 241–242
Active listening
   to false accusations, 158
   to feedback, 133–134
   method for, 120–123
   when telling your side of the
    story, 161–162
Adults. *See also specific types, e.g.:*
   Teachers hassles with, 148, 155,
    157–164, 169
   seeking help from, 130, 131, 155
   standing up for yourself with,
    124, 130, 131
Aerobic exercise, 209
Aggressive behavior and
   responses, 89, 125–127
Allegheny General Hospital, 258
"Always," in You-messages, 118
American Academy of Child and
   Adolescent Psychiatry, 257
American Academy of Sleep
   Medicine, 257
American Heart Association, 207
American Insomnia Association,
   257
American Professional Society on
   the Abuse of Children, 258
American Psychiatric Association,
   257

American Psychological Association, 234, 257

Anger. *See also specific topics, e.g.*:
ABCs of Anger and conflict staircase, 149
defined, 1–2
dietary irritants of, 206–207
fuel for, 2–8
mind and body connection for, 203
as normal emotion, 1, 9
pluses and minuses of, 29–33, 37
problems created by, 237, 239
and self-esteem, 178–179
standing up for yourself with, 124–125
taking ownership of, v–vi
turning off, 2
words you use to describe, 114–116

Anger cycle, 18–19, 240–242

Anger engine, 13, 14, 39–40, 115. *See also* ABCs of Anger

Anger level
on anger thermometer, 27–29, 152
description and experience of, 114–116
fluctuations in, 224
menstrual cycle and, 217–219
self-talk to reduce, 56
and walking away, 151, 152

Anger management benefits of, vii
deciding to seek help with, 228
difficulty with, v
Heads-Up Plan for practicing, 244–248
physical health and, 203
reasons for problems with, 229–230
reflection and recording to improve, 36
seeing a psychotherapist for help with, 231

Anger rumination, 15, 89–90. *See also* Stop the Drum Beat tools

Anger signals, 19–29
and anger thermometer, 27–29
benefits of knowing, 37
early warning signs of anger, 11, 239–241
in Hassle Plans, 165
scanning body and mind for, 20–27

Anger thermometer, 27–29, 152

Anger thinking traps, 54–67
Binocular Vision, 60–61
Black-or-White, 63–64
End of the World, 65, 66
Fallacy of Fairness, 61–62, 67
Fortune Telling, 64, 66
identifying, 66–67, 88
Jumping to Conclusions, 57–60, 65, 67
Justification, 66
The Line, 62
Mind Reading, 64–65
Need to Be Right, 66–67
Overgeneralization, 65
Shoulds, Need-Tos, and Have-Tos, 61–63
thought experiment on, 56

Anger triggers
foods and substances as, 207–208
in Heads-Up Plan, 239
on ICCAN form, 145
situations as, 48

Angry actions. See Actions, angry
Angry body. See Body, angry
Angry moments, as part of life, 251
Angry thoughts. See Thoughts, angry
Annoying habits, of peers, 149, 155
Antecedents of Anger, 12–13, 18, 19
Anxiety
  anger as mask for, 230
  readings for parents about, 256
  response to anger vs., v–vi
  and self-doubt, 174
Anxiety and Depression
  Association of America, 234, 257
Apologizing
  giving sincere apologies, 159–160
  as possible solution, 140, 141
  and telling your side of the story, 161
Apply a solution step (ICCAN method), 143
Arbitrary limits, setting, 62
Ask, in DEAL method, 128
Asking for what you want, 175
Asking questions, in ICCAN method, 139, 140, 143
Assertiveness
  angry helpful thoughts to encourage, 54
  in hassles with peers, 153
  responding to conflict with, 125–127
Association for Behavioral and Cognitive Therapies, 234, 256
Assumptions, checking, 121–123
Attention, 16, 121, 133–134
Attention-deficit-hyperactivity disorder, readings about, 256

Automatic problem-solving programs, 138–139
Automatic relaxation, 40, 47
Automatic thoughts, 21
Avoidance, 140,141, 152–153
Awareness, 21, 94, 106

Bad outcomes, gratitude for avoiding, 190
Balanced diet, 206
Basics of Anger, 13–14, 18, 19, 37
Beck Institute for Cognitive Behavior Therapy, 234, 257
Binocular Vision thinking trap, 60–61
Black-or-White thinking trap, 63–64
Blame
  for anger, vi
  and asking for help, 224
  by people with low self-esteem, 178
  sharing responsibility vs. blaming, 80–82
  and telling your side of the story, 161
Blood pressure, high, 208
Blood sugar, low, 208
Body, angry, 39–51
  in anger cycle, 19
  in Basics of Anger, 12–14
  counting to ten to calm, 46–47
  inner calm space in, 45–46
  during menstrual cycle, 215–217
  practicing calming tools, 49–51, 240–241
  preparing to calm, 40–41
  relaxing, 42–45

slow deep breathing to calm, 41–42, 46–49, 51

STOP as relaxation cue for, 47–49, 51

using ICCAN tool with, 145

Body language, 116–117, 120, 150, 164

Body scan, 20–26, 48, 191

Body signals of anger
on anger thermometer, 28
as early anger warning sign, 238
identifying, 20–21, 25–27
knowing, 37

Brain
effect of exercise on, 209
effect of sleep/wake schedule on, 215
survival response and, 2

Brainstorming possible solutions, 140

Breath2Relax app, 259

Breathing
in body scan for anger signals, 25
to calm angry body, 41–42, 46–48, 51
in gratitude meditation, 191
in self-acceptance meditation, 186–187

Bullseye choices, 144

Bullying, 155, 257

Caffeine, 207

Calcium, 206

Calm Body tools
counting to ten, 46–49, 51
finding inner calm space, 45–46
in Hassle Plans, 165
in Heads-Up Plan, 240–241

to help cool thoughts, 67
practicing using, 49–50
preparing to use, 40–41
progressive muscle relaxation, 42–45, 47–49
as remedies, 242, 243
slow deep breathing, 41–42, 46–49, 51
STOP as relaxation cue, 47–49, 51

Calories, in food, 204–205

Cardiovascular workout, 209

CARES Institute, 258

Caring, 101–107, 180–185

Center for Traumatic Stress in Children and Adolescents, 258

Change, in DEAL method, 128

Child Abuse Research Education Service, 258

Choices, in ICCAN method, 142–144

Clarification, 121–123, 134, 158

Coaches
anger and relationships with, 162
standing up for yourself with, 124, 130

Cognitive behavior therapy, 256–257

Communication
for dealing with false accusations, 158
for defusing conflict, 150
and self-esteem, 181

Communication tools, 113–137
Express Anger Effectively, 114–120
in Hassle Plans, 165
in Heads-Up Plan, 240–241

Listen Actively, 120–123
Negotiate a Compromise, 134–137, 141, 143
as remedies, 242, 243
Stand Up for Yourself, 124–131
Take Feedback Effectively, 132–135
Comparisons, 180, 198–199
Compassion
for others, 98–99, 112
self-, 103–107, 112, 181
Compliments
ability to accept, 174
defusing conflict with, 150
focusing on, in feedback, 134
as vaccine against hassles, 162, 164
Compromise, 133–136, 140, 141
Concentration, 15
Confidence
self-, 170, 171, 177–178, 200, 237
in using Hassle Plan, 168
Confidentiality, 235
Conflict, 147–169
with adults, 154, 156–163
body language when resolving, 116–117
communication habits that escalate, 114
defusing, 150
and Need to Be Right thinking trap, 66
negotiating a compromise to end, 134–135
passive, aggressive, and assertive responses to, 125–127
with peers, 149, 151–156
plans for dealing with, 164–168
You- vs. I-messages in, 118–119
Conflict staircase
described, 147–149
Hassle Plans to climb down, 169
in hassles with adults, 158, 159
and ignoring hassles, 151
Connection, strength of, 121
Consequences
of Anger, 16–18
in anger cycle, 18, 19
on ICCAN form, 142
in ICCAN method, 143
thinking ahead about, 83–85
Consider consequences step (ICCAN method), 143
Consider solutions step (ICCAN method), 139–143
Convenience foods, 206–207
COOL-CALM breathing exercise, 41–42, 46–47
Cool Thinking tools, 67–88
for defusing conflict, 149
Find the Facts, 68–71
in Hassle Plans, 165
in Heads-Up Plan, 240–241
Move to Another Seat, 72, 74–79
as remedies, 242, 243
Share a Slice of the Responsibility Pie, 79–82
Think It Through to the End, 82–85
Time Machine, 70–74
Write a Cool Letter to Your Hot-Tempered Self, 85–87
Cool words, for describing situations, 115
Core values, 34–36
Counting to ten, 46–49, 451
Creativity, as core value, 34, 35
Criticism

fogging method for dealing with, 133
in self-talk, 194–195
sensitivity to, 173–174
and writing a caring letter to yourself, 181–185

Dairy foods, 204–205
DEAL method, 128–130, 131, 136, 153
Defensiveness, 118–119, 132–134
Denial, 224–225
Depression
  anger as mask for, 229
  and asking for help, 225
  experiencing anger vs., 2
  as fuel for anger, 6
  readings for parents about, 256
  response to anger vs., v–vi
Describe, in DEAL method, 128
Detail, in gratitude journal, 189
Dismissive comments, 118
Distancing techniques, 92
Distract Yourself tool, 91, 112
Doctors of psychiatric medicine, 230
Doubt, self-, 171–173
Drumbeat of anger, 15. See also Stop the Drum Beat tools

Early anger warning signs, 11, 238–240
Eating habits, healthy, 203–204
Eating plan, 203
Educational psychologists, 230–231
Electronic devices, in wind-down routine, 214
Embarrassment, 2–3, 32

Emotion(s). See also Feelings
  anger as normal, 1, 9
  and gratitude journaling, 189
  in gratitude meditation, 191, 194
Emotional hurt. See Hurt feelings
End of the World thinking trap, 65, 66
Energy, to learn techniques, 229
Exaggeration, 176
Exercise, 208–211, 220
  aerobic, 208
  decline in, with age, 208–209
  and effects of menstrual cycle, 216
  from fun activities, 209, 210
  in health plan, 219
  physical activity and portion size, 204
Expectations, 61–63
Experiences, power of words to describe, 114–116
Experts, seeking help from, 223, 225–227
Express, in DEAL method, 128
Express Anger Effectively tool, 114–120
Expressing anger, 114–120
  benefits of, vi–vii, 33
  body language for, 116–117
  mixed signals when, 120
  using I-messages, 118–120
  words choice for clear communication, 117–118
  words used to describe anger, 114–116
Eye contact, 117

Face-to-face meetings, negotiating in, 135
Facial expression, 116, 120, 152
Facts, feelings and opinions vs., 68–71
Failure, 173–175
Fairness
  assertively seeking, 125–127
  making fair comparisons, 198–199
  solving problems related to, 138
  thinking trap about, 61–62, 67
  when negotiating a compromise, 135
Fallacy of Fairness thinking trap, 61–62, 67
False accusations, 157–159
Family, core values related to, 35
Family members
  anger and relationships with, 31, 162
  learning to express anger from, 7
  self-esteem of, 178–179
  sincere apologies to, 160
Fast food, 206–207
FDA (Food and Drug Administration), 206, 258
Fear, anger secondary to, 2, 3
Feedback, 127, 134–136, 173–174, 178
Feelings. See also Emotion(s); Hurt feelings
  expressing, in DEAL method, 128
  facts vs., 69–71
  noticing, in Watch the Drumbeat tool, 92
  pleasant, savoring, 99–100

rumination as intensifier of, 90–91
Fight-or-flight response, 1–2
Financial costs of anger, 31
Find the Facts tool, 68–72
Find the Good Thing in Someone tool, 101, 102
Flexibility, 62, 217
Fogging method, 133–134
Food allergies, 207–208
Food and Drug Administration (FDA), 207, 258
Food groups, 204
Food labels, 205–206
Forgive tool, 107–111
Fortune Telling thinking trap, 64, 66
Friends
  anger and relationships with, 30, 162
  practicing active listening with, 123
  standing up for yourself with, 124
  using Find the Facts tool with, 71
Friendship, as core value, 34, 35
Frowning, 116
Frustration, 5, 49, 145, 215–216
Fun activities, 91, 209, 210
Future, predicting, 64

Getting what you want, anger for, vi–vii, 33
Gift mindset, 190–192
Gluten, 205
Goals, considering others', 76–79
Good attributes of others, finding, 101, 102
Gratitude, meditating on, 190–194

Gratitude journals, 188–190
Guilt, 5, 32, 174–175

Habit(s)
  anger rumination as, 90
  annoying, of peers, 149, 155
  building, 167
  changing, 34
  falling into old, 238
  healthy eating, 203–204
  healthy sleep, 215–216, 218
Hangry, being, 208
Happify app, 258
Harvard University, 205
Hassle Plans, 147
  assertiveness tools in, 153
  building, 164–166, 169
  Hassle Plan ladder, 167
  and ignoring hassles, 152
  Peer, 155, 156
  practicing, 167–169
  using successful solutions in, 144
Hassles
  with adults, 155, 157–164, 169
  with peers, 149, 151–156, 169
  vaccinating yourself against, 162, 164
Have-Tos, as rules for situations, 63
Headaches, food allergies and, 207–208
Headspace app, 259
Heads-Up Plan, 238–253
  anger cycle and tools list, 240–241
  building, 242, 244–245
  early anger warning signs on, 238–239

example, 247–249
form for, 251–253
practicing managing anger with, 245–246
risks and remedies, 241–243
Health plan, developing, 217, 219
Healthy Eating Plate, 205
Help, seeking
  to assert yourself, 131, 121
  from experts, 223, 225–227
  in hassles with peers, 155
  as possible solution to problem, 140, 141
  from a professional, 223–236
  reasons given for not, 224–226
Helpful thoughts, 54
Hidden motives, 75, 79
High blood pressure, 208
High self-esteem, 172
Honesty, in stand-up sandwich, 131
Hope, 237
Hopelessness, 224
Hormonal imbalance, 216
Hot thoughts, 67
Hot words, 115
Humor, 96–97
Hurt, physical, 3, 177, 188
Hurt feelings
  as fuel for anger, 3
  ouch-anger arc for, 177
  and passive response to conflict, 127
  for people with low self-esteem, 8, 173–174, 200
  self-acceptance and, 185
Hypoglycemia, 208

ICCAN problem solving method, 137–145
  about, 138–139
  apply a solution step, 143
  consider consequences step, 143
  consider solutions step, 139–143
  developing Peer Hassle Plan with, 155
  identifying the problem, 138–145
  identify the problem step, 139, 140
  now review step, 144–145
  using, when frustrated or angry, 145
Identify the problem step (ICCAN method), 139, 140
Ignoring hassles, 151–152
Images
  in body scan for anger signals, 22–25
  calming body with positive imagery, 45–46, 49, 51
  as early anger warning signal, 238
  as fuel for anger, 14–15
I-messages, using, 118–120
Inner calm space, finding, 45–46. *See also* Positive imagery
Intentions, guessing at others, 64–65
International OCD Foundation, 256
International Society for Traumatic Stress Studies, 258
Interruptions, 149
Irritability, 6, 207–208, 216–217
I-statements, 118–120, 162

Job loss, anger-related, 31
Journaling
  gratitude journal, 188–190
  sleep diary, 212–213
  with Write It Down tool, 93
Judgment, 2
Jumping to Conclusions thinking trap, 58–61, 65, 67
Justification thinking trap, 66

Khrushchev, Nikita, 114

Labels, for people, 60
Laugh a Little tool, 96–97
LCSWs (licensed clinical social workers), 231
Letters to yourself
  caring, 180–185
  from cool to hot-tempered self, 85–87
  of recommendation, 194–197
  to stop drumbeat of anger, 92–93
Licensed clinical social workers (LCSWs), 231
Licensed professional counselors (LPCs), 231
Liking yourself, 195–202
  letters of recommendation for yourself, 195–199
  making fair comparisons, 198–199
  savoring the good about yourself, 198–199
The Line thinking trap, 62
List, in DEAL method, 128
Listen Actively tool, 120–123
Listening

active, 120–123, 133–134, 158, 161–162
  and anger rumination, 15
  to deal with false accusations, 158
Lists, of good stuff about yourself, 197–198
Loving-kindness meditation, 103–107
Low blood sugar, 208
Low self-confidence, 170–171
Low self-esteem
  anger fueled by, 7–8
  effects of, 170
  factors in, 178–180
  methods of improving, 181–199
  signs of, 172–177
LPCs (licensed professional counselors), 231

Magnifying thinking trap, 59
Marriage and family therapists (MFTs), 231
Media messages, self-esteem and, 180
Medical testing, in psychotherapy, 234–235
Medical University of South Carolina, 258
Medication, 235, 256
Meditation
  on gratitude, 190–193
  loving-kindness, 103–107
  scanning body for anger signals, 20–26
  on self-acceptance, 185–188
  in Surf the Drum Beat of Anger exercise, 94
Memories, 12, 99–100

Menstrual cycle, 215–217
Mental actions, angry, 15
Mental health professional(s)
  finding a, 231–232
  frequently asked questions about, 232–235
  online resources on, 256–257
  preparing to meet with, 234
  types of, 230–231
Messages
  buying in to, 200
  from family members, 178–180
  I- and You-, 118–120, 162
  from media, 180
  repeating, 121–122, 132, 134, 158
  rewording, 132–133
  with shame vs. guilt, 5
  from yourself, 180
MFTs (marriage and family therapists), 231
Middle ground, finding, 134–135
Mind and body connection, for anger, 202
The Mindfulness App, 259
Mind Reading thinking trap, 64–65
Mind scan, in gratitude meditation, 191
Mind signals of anger
  on anger thermometer, 28
  identifying, 20–21, 25–27
  knowing, 37
Minimization, problem, 224–225
Misdirection, anger as, 5
Mistakes, 157, 160, 176
Misunderstandings, 121–122, 134, 138
Mixed signals, in communication, 120

Mobile apps, 258–259
Moderation, eating in, 206
Mood, menstrual cycle and, 216
Motivator, anger as, 138
Motives of others, 58–59, 75–76, 78
Move to Another Seat tool, 72, 74–79
"Must," in You-messages, 118
My Mood Tracker app, 258

Name calling, 152
National Child Traumatic Stress Network, 258
National Crime Victims Research and Treatment Center, 258
National Institute of Mental Health (NIMH), 258
National Institutes of Health (NIH), 207, 258
National Sleep Foundation (NSF), 217, 257
Need to Be Right thinking trap, 66–67
"Need to," in You-messages, 118
Need-Tos, as rules for situations, 62–63
Negative attributes
    in Black-or-White thinking trap, 63–64
    focusing on, when taking feedback, 132
    writing caring letters to yourself about, 182–186
Negotiate a Compromise tool, 134–135, 141–143
Neutral thoughts, 54
"Never," in You-messages, 118
Nice comments, in stand-up sandwich, 130–131

NIH (National Institutes of Health), 207, 258
NIMH (National Institute of Mental Health), 258
"No," saying, 175
Now review step (ICCAN method), 144–145
NSF (National Sleep Foundation), 217, 257
Nutrition, 202–209, 221
    balanced diet, 205
    caffeine, sugar, and other anger irritants, 208–209
    calorie-dense foods, 204–205
    eating from food groups, 204
    and effects of menstrual cycle, 218
    in fast food and convenience meals, 207–208
    in health plan, 224
    healthy eating habits, 207–208
    healthy eating plan, 207
    information on food labels, 209–210
    physical activity and portion size, 209
Nutrition Facts food labels, 205–206

Objects, gratitude for, 191
Online resources, 256–258
Opinions, facts vs., 68
Organized sports, 209–211
Ouch-anger arc, 174, 178, 186
Overgeneralization thinking trap, 65
Over-the-top compliments, 163
Ownership, of anger, v–vi

Paraphrasing, 122
Parents
    anger and relationships with, 31, 162
    false accusations by, 157–158
    help in changing sleep habits from, 217
    readings for, 256
    sharing Heads-Up Plan with, 245
    sincere apologies to, 161
    standing up for yourself to, 124
    using Find the Facts tool with, 71
Passive responses to conflict, 125–127
Pay It Forward app, 259
Peer Hassle Plans, 155–156
Peers, hassles with, 148–156, 169
People, gratitude for, 189–190, 192–195
Perfectionism, 66, 175
Personal space, 117
Perspective, changing, 72, 75–76
Pessimism, 175
Pets, gratitude for, 192
Physical actions, angry, 15, 89. See also actions, angry
Physical activity, 209. See also Exercise
Physical exams, 235–236
Physical health, 202–221
    and anger during menstrual cycle, 217–219
    core values related to, 35
    developing health plan, 219–220
    exercise, 209–212
    nutrition, 202–209
    online resources, 256–257
    and self-esteem, 181
    sleep quality, 212–215, 221

Physical hurt, 3
Physical signs of anger. See Body, angry
Pizza to pizza exercise, 200
Planning ahead, 82–84
Play, core values related to, 35
Pleasant feelings, savoring, 99–100
Portion size, 205
Positive imagery, 45–46, 50–51
Postponing anger rumination, 95–96
Practice Caring and Compassion Toward Yourself tool, 103–107
Practicing, 228–229
    active listening, 122
    Calm Body tools, 50
    Cool Body tools, 40
    Hassle Plans, 168
    Heads-Up Plan, 245–246
    liking yourself, 194, 200
    self-acceptance, 200
    STOP relaxation cue, 47–48
Praise, 195
Predicting the future, 64
Privacy, 236
Problem
    anger as a signal of, 138
    clarifying, 122–123, 158
    describing, 128, 150
    identifying, 139–140
    listing how change will fix, 128
    minimizing, 225–226
Problem solving. See also ICCAN problem solving method
    anger and, 137–138
    asking for help as part of, 224–227
    communication in, 113, 117

and self-esteem, 181
tools for, in Hassle Plans, 165
using anger in, 137–138
Professional associations, mental
health, 257
Professional help, 223–236
determining when to seek,
224–237
frequently asked questions
about, 228–234
from mental health
professionals, 231–235
from psychotherapists, 231–235
reasons people don't seek,
229–230
Progressive muscle relaxation,
43–45, 47–48
Psychiatrists (doctors of
psychiatric medicine), 231
Psychological symptoms, with
menstrual cycle, 217–219
Psychologists, 231–232
Psychology Today, 234
Psychotherapist(s), 231–235
benefits of seeing, 231, 237
changing, 237
finding a, 232–233
frequently asked questions
about, 235–237
number of sessions with, 236–
237
preparing to meet with, 235
sharing Heads-Up Plan with, 245
Put-downs, 118, 147, 151–152, 176.
See also Conflict

Rationalization, of behavior, 66
Recording
of ABCs of anger, 12–17

of core values, 36
to identify early anger warning
signs, 11
to improve responses to anger,
37
Reflection (reflecting)
for anger management, 37
on core values, 35–37
on early anger warning signs, 11
in gratitude meditation, 191–195
on level of anger, 27–29
on pluses and minuses of anger,
29–33
scanning mind and body for
anger, 20–27
with Write It Down tool, 93–94
Relationships
effect of anger on, 30–31, 162
misunderstandings in, 120
Relaxation
to calm angry body, 39–40
progressive muscle, 42–45, 47–49
STOP as cue for, 47–49, 51
with Watch the Drumbeat tool,
92–93
Remedies, in Heads-Up Plan,
242–243
Repeating message
in active listening, 121–122, 158
when standing up for yourself,
133
when taking in feedback, 133
Requests, making, 126, 130–131
Resentment, 64, 108, 109, 111
Respect, 124–125
Responsibility, sharing, 79–82
Reviewing solution, in ICCAN
method, 144–145
Rewording messages, 121–122

Right, need to be, 66–67
Risks, in Heads-Up Plan, 242–243
Rule of thirds, 205
Rules for situations, setting up,
	62–63
Rumination, anger, 15, 89–91. *See
	also* Stop the Drum Beat tools
Rumors, spreading, 149, 155

Sadness, anger secondary to, 2, 3
Sarcasm, 118, 120
Saving face, 152–153
Savor the Good and Pleasant tool,
	99–100, 198–199
Schedule, sleep, 214–215
Schedule Drum Practice tool,
	95–96, 112
School, 31, 35
Self-acceptance, 18–200
	keeping a gratitude journal,
		189–191
	meditating on, 186–189
	and meditating on gratitude,
		190–195
	script for, 187–189
	writing caring letters to
		yourself, 182–186
Self-compassion, 101–107, 112, 181
Self-confidence
	defined, 170
	and hope, 238
	importance of, 201
	and self-esteem, 178–179
	and success in life, 171
Self-doubt, 171–174
Self-esteem, 170–201
	anger and, 178–179
	defined, 170
	factors in, 179–181

as fuel for anger, 7–8
methods of boosting, 182–200
and self-doubt, 171–172
signs of, 172–177
and success in life, 171
Self-esteem tree, 179–180
Self-image, 32–33
Self-talk, 58, 63, 181, 195
Sensations, 21–25, 45–46
Setbacks, response to, 201
Shame, 3, 5, 175–176, 225
Share a Slice of the Responsibility
	Pie tool, 79–82
"Should," in You-messages,
	118–120
Shoulds, Need-Tos, and Have-Tos
	thinking trap, 62–63
Shrinking thinking trap, 61
Significant other, effects of anger
	on, 30
Sincerity
	in apologies, 158–160
	delivering compliments with,
		163
	in stand-up sandwich, 131
Sleep, 212–217, 221
	anger and problems with, 31–32
	effects of chronic lack of, 212
	and effects of menstrual cycle,
		217
	and food allergies, 208–209
	in health plan, 220
	healthy sleep habits, 215–216,
		219–220
	online resources on, 257
	wind-down routine, 215
Sleep diary, 213–214
Sleep schedule, 214–215
Sleep tank, low, 213

Slow deep breathing, 41–42, 47, 51
Smiling, 116
Social media, 181
Solution(s)
  applying, 142–144
  choosing best, 142, 145
  considering, 140–143
  modifying, 144
  possible, 145
  reviewing, 144–145
  when negotiating a
  compromise, 134–137
Space for others, creating, 117
Specificity, in gratitude journal,
  190
Sports, 35, 209
Standing up for yourself, 124–131
  with DEAL method, 128–129, 137
  knowing your rights, 124–125
  passive, aggressive, and
  assertive responses, 125–127
  repeating requests, 133
Stand Up for Yourself tool, 124–131
Stand-up sandwich, 130–131
STOP relaxation cue, 47–49, 51
Stop the Drum Beat tools, 89–112
  Distract Yourself, 91
  Find the Good Thing in
  Someone, 101, 102
  Forgive, 107–112
  in Hassle Plans, 165
  in Heads-Up Plan, 239–241
  Laugh a Little, 96–98
  Practice Caring and Compassion
  Toward Yourself, 101–107
  as remedies, 242–243
  Savor the Good and Pleasant,
  99–100, 198–199
  Schedule Drum Practice, 95–96

Walk a Minute in Their Shoes,
  98–99
  Watch the Drumbeat, 92, 94
  when walking away, 152–153
  Write It Down, 93–95
Story, telling your side of, 160–162
Strengths, liking your, 200
Stress
  in body, 39
  as effect of anger, 31–32
  with End of the World thinking
  trap, 65
  as fuel for anger, 2, 4, 31, 18
  and menstrual cycle, 217
  with over-focusing on
  accomplishments, 173
  progressive muscle relaxation to
  release, 42–45
  response to anger vs., v–vi
Survival response, anger in, 1–2
Swear words, 118

Take Feedback Effectively tool, 133
Talking too much, 161
T-charts, 69, 134–135
Teachers
  anger and relationships with,
  31, 161
  false accusations by, 157–158
  sincere apologies to, 160
  standing up for yourself with,
  124, 130
Teasing, 149, 155
Teens
  causes of anger for, 9
  consequences of acting badly
  for, 83
  decline in exercise for, 209–211

growth and healthy eating for, 203–209

readings for, 255

rights of, 124, 136

sleep required by, 212

Telling your side of the story, 160–162

Tension, 4, 39, 43

Thanking people, for feedback, 134

Thinking

acting before, 84

effect of anger on, 47, 138–139

Thinking ahead, 82–84

Think It Through to the End tool, 82–85

Thirds, rule of, 205

Thought actions, angry, 15

Thoughts, angry, 53–88

in anger cycle, 19

anger thinking traps associated with, 68

in Basics of Anger, 13–15

changing, to cool thoughts, 67–87

cool thoughts vs., 58

as early warning signal, 239

Find the Facts tool for cooling, 68–72

helpful, neutral, and unhelpful, 54

identifying anger thinking traps, 54–67

Move to Another Seat tool for cooling, 72, 74–79

noticing, in Watch the Drumbeat tool, 92–93

practicing calming tools, 241–242

scanning mind for anger, 20–27

Share a Slice of the Responsibility Pie tool for cooling, 79–82

Think It Through to the End tool for cooling, 82–85

Time Machine tool for cooling, 68, 72–74

using ICCAN tool with, 145

Write a Cool Letter to Your Hot-Tempered Self tool for cooling, 85–87

Thoughts, in body scan for anger signals, 21–25

Time

gaining perspective over, 72–74

to learn to techniques, 229

Time Machine tool, 72–73

Timing, of compliments, 164

To yourself, to build self-esteem, 181–185

To yourself, to stop drumbeat of anger, 92–93

Trauma, dealing with, 258

True accusations, 158–164

Truth, 68–72, 161

Tunnel vision, 101

Understanding, with forgiveness, 110

Unexpected events, 191

Unhelpful thoughts, 54

United Nations, 114

Unrealistic goals, 176

Unreasonable requests, 129

Urges, as angry thoughts, 15

Vacation, following health plan on, 219

Verbal provocations, responses to, 149–168

Visualization, 167, 187–189

Vitamins, 206

Voice, calm, 117

Walk a Minute in Their Shoes tool, 98–99

Walking away, 152–153

Warning signs, 11, 239–241

Watch the Drumbeat tool, 92–93

Weaknesses, accepting, 200

Weekends, sleeping in on, 214–215

Wellbeing, core values related to, 35

Wind-down routine, 215

The Wizard of Oz (film), 34

Women, physical/psychological symptoms of menstrual cycle, 217–219

Words
  angry, possible solutions involving, 140–141
  communicating clearly with, 117–120
  for describing anger, 114–116
  matching body language and, 120

Work, 31, 35

Workout, cardiovascular, 209

World Health Organization, 204

Worry, 32, 65

Write a Cool Letter to Your Hot-Tempered Self tool, 85–87

Write It Down tool, 93–94

You-messages, 118–120, 161

Zero-to-sixty anger, v
  actions associated with, 15
  communication for people with, 113
  conflict and, 114, 168
  consequences of, 142
  early warning signs of, 11
  effects of, 1
  Hassle Plans to prevent, 164–167
  help learning to cool, 249
  Jumping to Conclusions and, 57–60
  low self-esteem and, 171
  minuses of, 30–32
  responses to verbal hassles by people with, 151
  slip ups in dealing with, 223–224
  thinking traps for people with, 54–67
  tools for getting a handle on, 223–224
  unhelpful angry thoughts in, 54
  ups and downs of dealing with, 251
  usual anger vs., 1, 9

ACKNOWLEDGEMENTS

There are several people who helped me keep my cool while writing this book. I thank my colleagues (Jonathan Barkin, Emily Berner, Joan Davidson, Daniela Owen, and Monique Thompson) at the San Francisco Bay Area Center for Cognitive Therapy. They're the calming and supportive harbor that is my professional home. I also thank Judy Beck and Jackie Persons for their inspiring support over the years. I'm fortunate to call these rock stars of cognitive behavior therapy my colleagues and friends.

I thank Kristine Enderle, editorial director of Magination Press, for her steady support of this book and for her unimaginable patience with one missed deadline after another. I also thank Katie ten Hagen for her thoughtful and clever suggestions. She greatly improved the quality of the book. I also thank the members of the Advisory Board of Magination Press and the American Psychological Association who reviewed early drafts of the manuscript. Their thoughtful remarks were invaluable.

I thank my partner, Luann DeVoss, for her unwavering support of this project and the many other things that take me away from home on weekends. I thank my daughters, Madeleine and Olivia, who are awesome young women in every way. I'm honored to be their dad.

Last, I thank the many teens and their parents who have come to me for help over the years. I thought of you often as I worked on the book and realized that I learned as much if not more from you than you learned from me. We were are a great team!

MICHAEL A. TOMPKINS, PHD, ABPP is a licensed psychologist and board certified in behavioral and cognitive psychology by the American Board of Professional Psychology. He is the co-director and co-founder of the San Francisco Bay Area Center for Cognitive Therapy, Assistant Clinical Professor at the University of California at Berkeley, and an adjunct faculty member for the Beck Institute for Cognitive Behavior Therapy. Dr. Tompkins serves on the Advisory Board of Magination Press. He is the author or co-author of 12 books, including *My Anxious Mind: A Teen's Guide to Managing Anxiety and Panic* (with Katherine Martinez), which is a Magination Press best seller and included in the Reading Well for Young People initiative sponsored by the Wellcome Trust, London, United Kingdom. He lives in Oakland, California. Visit him at sfbacct.com and on Twitter @drmatompkins.

CHLOE DOUGLASS works in her home studio to create illustrations, character designs, and story ideas. She graduated from Kingston University with an MA Illustration degree in 2012. She lives in Tooting, London. Visit her at chloeillustrates.co.uk, and on Twitter and Instagram @ChloeIllustrates.

MAGINATION PRESS is the children's book imprint of the American Psychological Association. Through APA's publications, the association shares with the world mental health expertise and psychological knowledge. Magination Press books reach young readers and their parents and caregivers to make navigating life's challenges a little easier. It's the combined power of psychology and literature that makes a Magination Press book special. Visit us at maginationpress.org and on Facebook, Twitter, Instagram, and Pinterest @MaginationPress.